Grandpa What Did You Do In "The Big War" - World War I:

You Mean "To Make The World Safe For Democracy" 1918 Letters

MALLETT
RESERVE
VETERANS
CLUB

Grandpa What Did You Do In "The Big War" - World War I: You Mean "To Make The World Safe For Democracy" 1918 Letters

Robert Newcomb Marling

Compiled by Roberta Marling Morris
Edited by Donald Wayne Downey

WWII Veterans History Fund
2019

First Printing: 2019

ISBN 978-1-63010-012-4

Library of Congress Control Number:2019907236

WWII Veteran History Fund
San Ramon, California
www.dondowney.com

Dedication

To the Memory of all of the WWI Veterans on the 100th Anniversary of the End of the "War to End All Wars"

Thanks. to WWI Veteran Robert Newcomb Marling, for writing so many letters home.

Contents

Acknowledgements ...ix
Foreward ... xi
Preface ... xiii
Forward ... xi
Preface...xiii
Introduction ... 1
Letters from Robert Newcomb Marling to home in USA...17-353

Acknowledgements

I would like to thank, Denise and Don Downey from the WWII Veterans History Fund, without whose help this book would never have been completed.

Thank you for your patience and guidance, your skill in assembling this book.

Foreword

Robert N. Marling was a 20 year old college student who volunteered on June 10, 1917 in the Red Cross in Evanston, IL to be an Ambulance driver before America entered World War I.

The volunteers trained on two ambulances in Evanston, staying in private homes until barracks were available in Fort Sheridan. This group of students, bus and taxi drivers were then assigned to the base at Chillicothe, Ohio and assigned to the American

Expeditionary Forces and sent to France in January 1918. They were assigned to the Reserve Mallet commanded by French General Richard Mallet to the Motor Truck Company 369 American Mission PROV. CD. D, POR B.C.M American EXPEDITIONARY FORCES, PARIS, FRANCE. Not many men were experienced truck drivers and maintenance mechanics.

The mission was to drive Pierce Arrow Trucks loaded with ammunition, supplies, guns, tanks and soldiers to the battle trenches. On the return to Base they treated and brought the wounded soldiers to receive medical care and also bring the dead back to be buried.

He was one of a few American soldiers who fought in Four Defensive Battles on the Western Front protecting the road to Paris and stopped the Germans and participated in the Four Offensive Battles over the same ground pushing the Germans back to the Somme and across the river to Sedan where the Germans surrendered and agreed to the Armistice on November 11, 1918.

He received the VICTORY MEDEL WITH 8 CLASPS AND ALSO EARNED A NINTH FOR HIS WORK REMAINING IN France hauling food and supplies and rehabilitating the towns, farms and battlefields in northern France. He returned to Camp Grant, Illinois on June 20, 1919.

Roberta Martling Morris
June 2019

Preface

We met Roberta at the Danville Veteran's Day Commemoration 2019 to remember the 100th Anniversary of the End of WWI. We interviewed Roberta at her display of her Dad's WWI Memorabilia and later visited her at her home and did and extensive interview.

Roberta has quite a collection of WWI letters home and we were privileged to scan the letters and make this First Edition, which we hope will lead to a more organized book with transcribed text of the letters in the future.

Denise & Don Downey
Editors

Introduction

A collection of over 150 letters to home from WWI soldier Robert Newcomb Marling, a volunteer to the American Expeditionary Forces, a formation of the United States Army on the Western Front of World War I. The AEF was established on July 5, 1917, in France under the command of Gen. John J. Pershing. WWI and family photos plus a collection of memorabilia and personal letters are included.

Roberta published the original book about her Dad. This volume includes that content and is part of an additional three-volume set of scanned letters, divided by year. The letters are sorted by date and separated by Roberta's notes, followed by scans of the envelopes and then the letters in the order of scanning. Robert Marling used all sides of the paper he had available, so one must follow his writing to locate the next section of the page he wrote on.

Denise & Don Downey
Editors

Jan 7/1918
Camp Merritt, NJ.

Aunt Amy sent $5 he bought
pair of Boots. with
Christmas money.

He is wrestling
Went shopping in New York
went to Theater + Dinners on
Broadway.
Celebrated his 21st B. Day at Yale Club

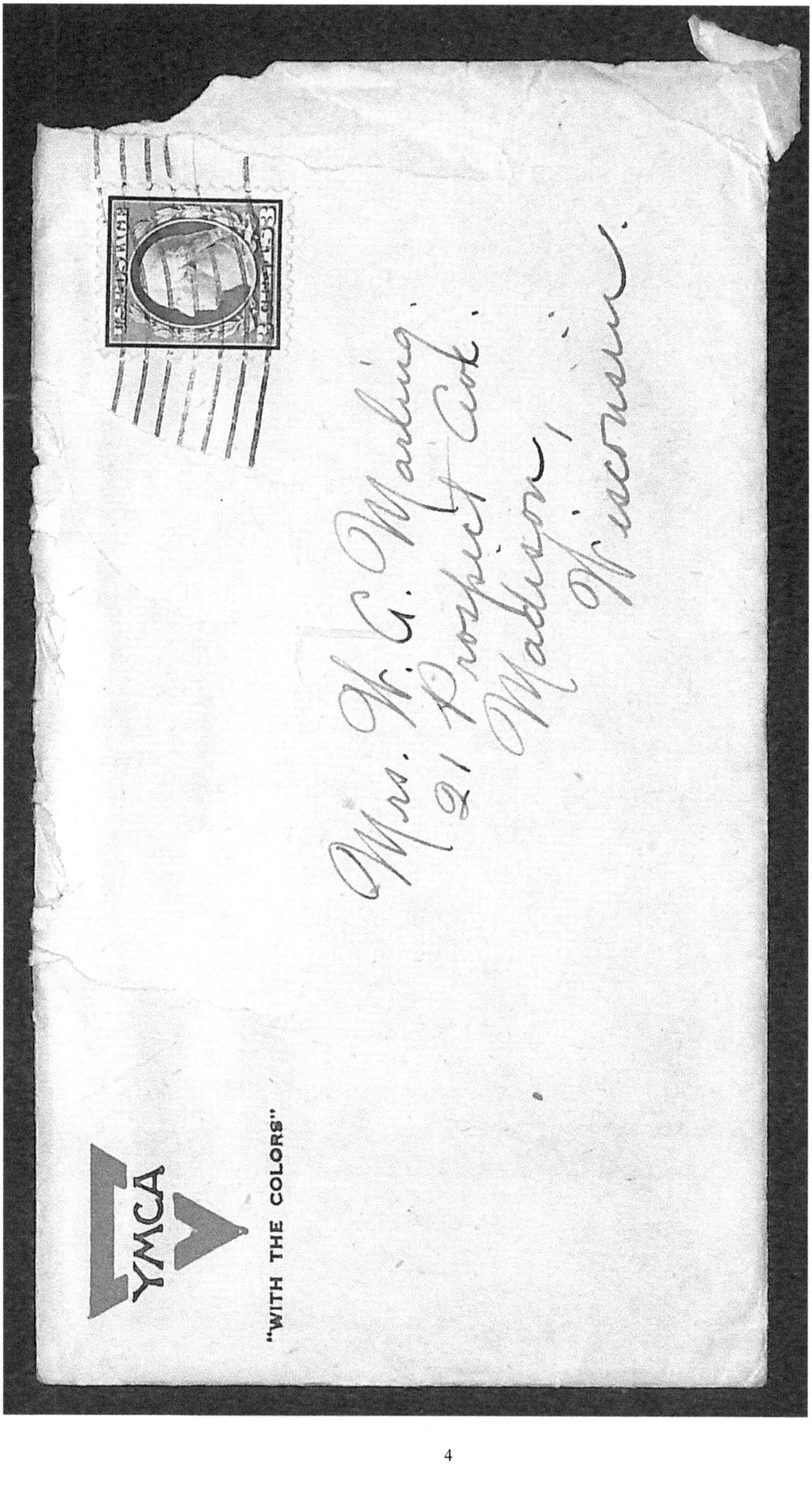
YMCA
"WITH THE COLORS"
21 Prospect Ave.
Madison,
Wisconsin.

"WITH THE COLORS" YMCA

Camp Merritt N.J.
Jan. 7th, 1918.

Dear Mother,

I just received your letter together with Margarets and Cecilia's. Where did you ever get the idea that Camp Merritt is in or near Jersey City? Camp Merritt is on a ridge between Dumont on the west and Cresskill and Tenafly on the east. My mail comes either thru Dumont or Tenafly but I notice on many of your letters you have Jersey City. I hear from Bill & Melo too and hearing from all of you at once was a great delight. Just had dinner and it was pretty good for a change. While I was at dinner a letter came from Shirly and a postal from Bill.

I am sorry to hear that you have been so ill and mighty

HELP YOUR COUNTRY BY SAVING. WRITE ON BOTH SIDES OF THIS PAPER

pleased that you are getting better. I heard that Bill too has been having trouble with a skinned shin.

I got Aunt Amy's candy and it surely was a great treat. I am still eating the hard candy and it ought to last several days longer. I must write and thank her when she gets home again, or if you see her first I wish you would give her my thanks and love. Tell her that I got a pair of boots with the Xmas money she gave me. They are mighty fine and ought to give splendid service.

Wrestling is a splendid sport and fine exercise to a person when in good condition and is very favorably looked upon by Army and Navy. There is no more danger in it than in any other sport and is not as taxing as basketball so don't worry about my overexerting myself. I let the other fellow work to throw me until he gets tired and then I usually get him.

"WITH THE COLORS" YMCA

Tell Aunt Amy that I can't very well accept her sweater as I am now pretty much loaded down with knitted goods. They sent me your helmet from Evanston and I have it packed away for future use.

Shurly McNamee is going into the Navy next month in the wireless department. Before he goes to sea he has to have a months training at Chicago and four months at Harvard. I'm mighty glad Shurly is getting into it and I'm proud of him, but it will be awfully hard on his mother and father.

Last Thursday and Saturday I went to New York. Thursday I did a little shopping getting things that were necessary

HELP YOUR COUNTRY BY SAVING. WRITE ON BOTH SIDES OF THIS PAPER

"WITH THE COLORS" YMCA

Sheridan at the last training camp. While there he broke his leg and is still quite a cripple and we had to help him back to the Yale Club, 43rd + 5th Ave. So I had quite a fine time on my twenty-first birthday anniv. I may go in again to see Marguerite either tomorrow or next day, provided our ship isn't coaled by that time.

Thursday at the theatre I ran onto Bob Wolfers and Pat Hayes, both Betas, Hayes is on Admiral Johnston's flag-ship, and Wolfers is still in school but just up here spending the holidays. He is engaged to Ruth Stromme I believe, one of Mary's friends.

HELP YOUR COUNTRY BY SAVING. WRITE ON BOTH SIDES OF THIS PAPER

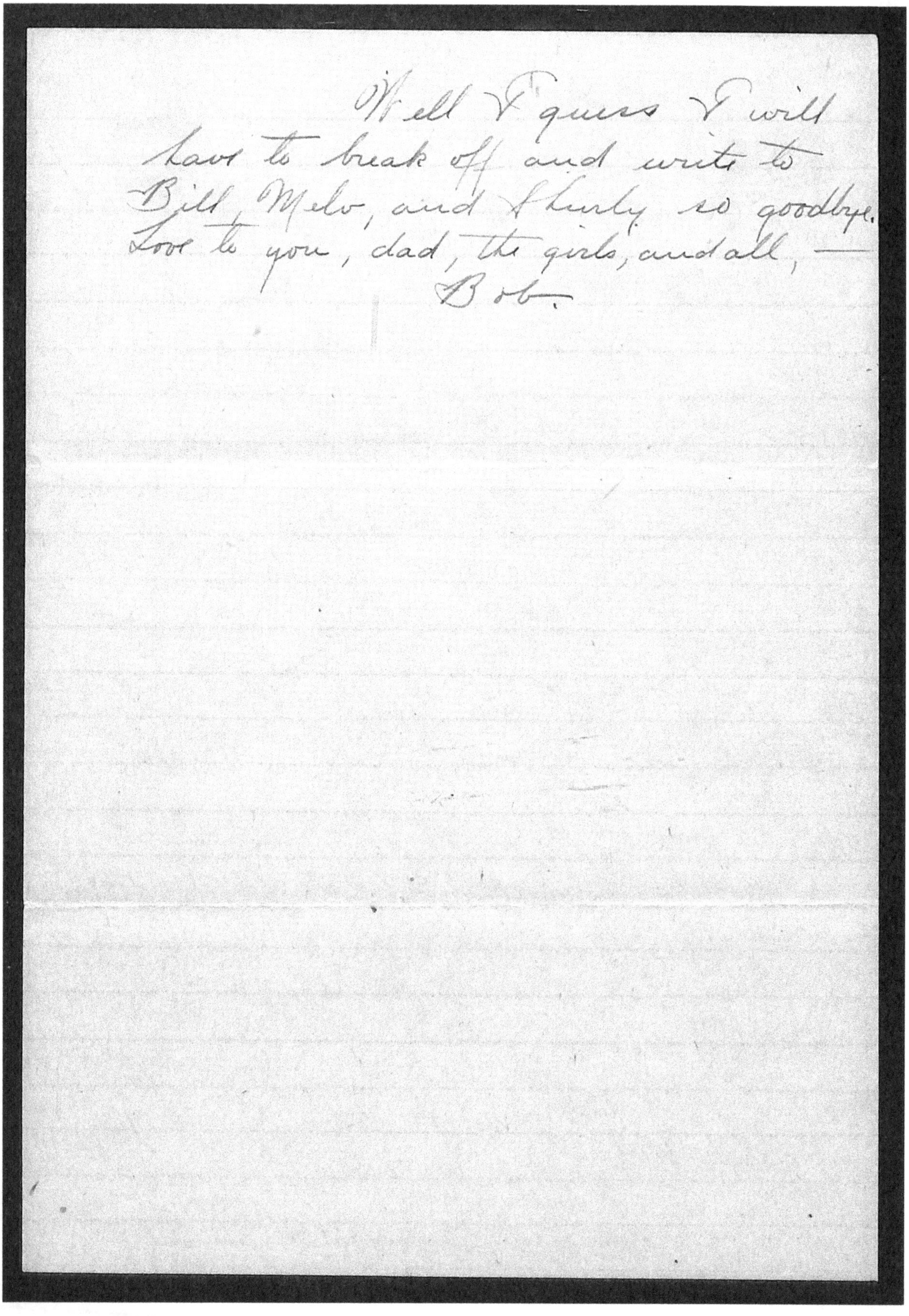
Well I guess I will
have to break off and write to
Bill, Melo, and Shirly so goodbye.
Love to you, dad, the girls, and all, —
Bob.

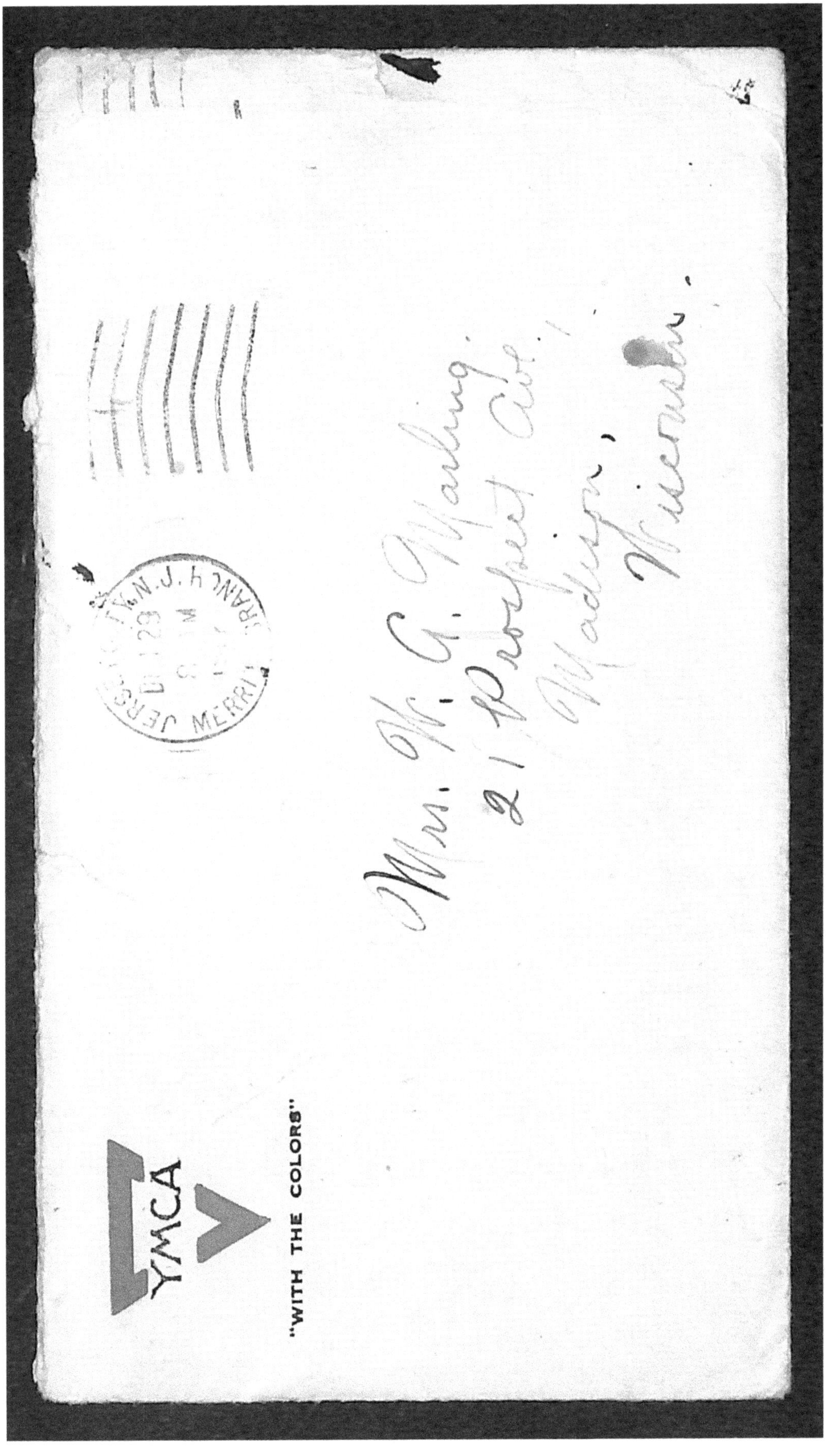
YMCA
"WITH THE COLORS"

Camp Merritt
Jan. 10, 1918.

Dear Mother,

You delighted me very much with your birthday letter. And tell Grandma Marling that I was very much pleased with the money and her kind wishes. It came just in time (the letter I mean) for it is likely that we pull out tomorrow and you already know what my address will be. We have been having a great deal of contagious disease in our battalion, two or more cases being carried away to the hospital today, one of the a case of diphtheria from our company. It would not surprise me a great deal to find the battalion again quarantined tomorrow.

I was very glad to hear that you are improving and hope you recover speedily. Thank you for the kindness of thot of sending me the food and realize how impossible it was to improve the impulse by action. I thank you and father very much for the $100, and hope that it will soon be drawing interest, as I may be able to use it when I get back.

When I was a kid I used to think what fun it would be to be a soldier. Every man in a uniform was soldier to me then and was a sort of hero to me. Its funny how ones views change as he grows older. Still the army is not all work and there are several features of the life

going into business and still I feel that I ought to go in with father and try to help him out. Which do you think would be better for me to do? I really don't know. I think that I could be of better service if I went to college a few years, but that would put off the time of my going in with dad.

I have written to Babe Thompson several times but haven't had an answer so I didn't know what he was doing until you wrote to me that he had to reenlist in something or other. If I had know he was interested I would have coaxed him into this outfit while we were still at Camp Sherman.

that I enjoy and that I can takeadvantage of. I never thought that there would be another war and that I would be in it at the age of twenty-one. But the war can't last forever and I am ever confident of coming back better fitted for a useful civil life.

I am very glad that I have been a joy to you and I will always try to give you joy and comfort and sometime make you proud of me. The thing that puzzels me very much is as to the course to take after I come home. I would like to get a better education before

~~[illegible]~~ I don't believe any one can be more pleased than I that Margaret is growing up and losing her flesh. I have looked for her to start getting slender for some time, and I had begun to think that she was going to stay stout.

Time is short and we are very busy just now so goodbye and goodluck, and <u>don't worry</u>. With all my love to you all,

Your Aff. Son.
Bob.

U.S. POSTAGE
3 CENTS 3
Mrs. H. G. Marling,
21 Prospect Ave.,
Madison,
Wisconsin.

Pvt. R. W. Marling
Soldiers Mail
U.S. FEB 1 6 PM 1918 POSTAL SERVICE
Mrs. W. A. Marling
21 Prospect Avenue,
Madison,
Wisconsin
CENSORED A.E.F.
O.K. Lieut. James Mulholland U.S.A.
#2

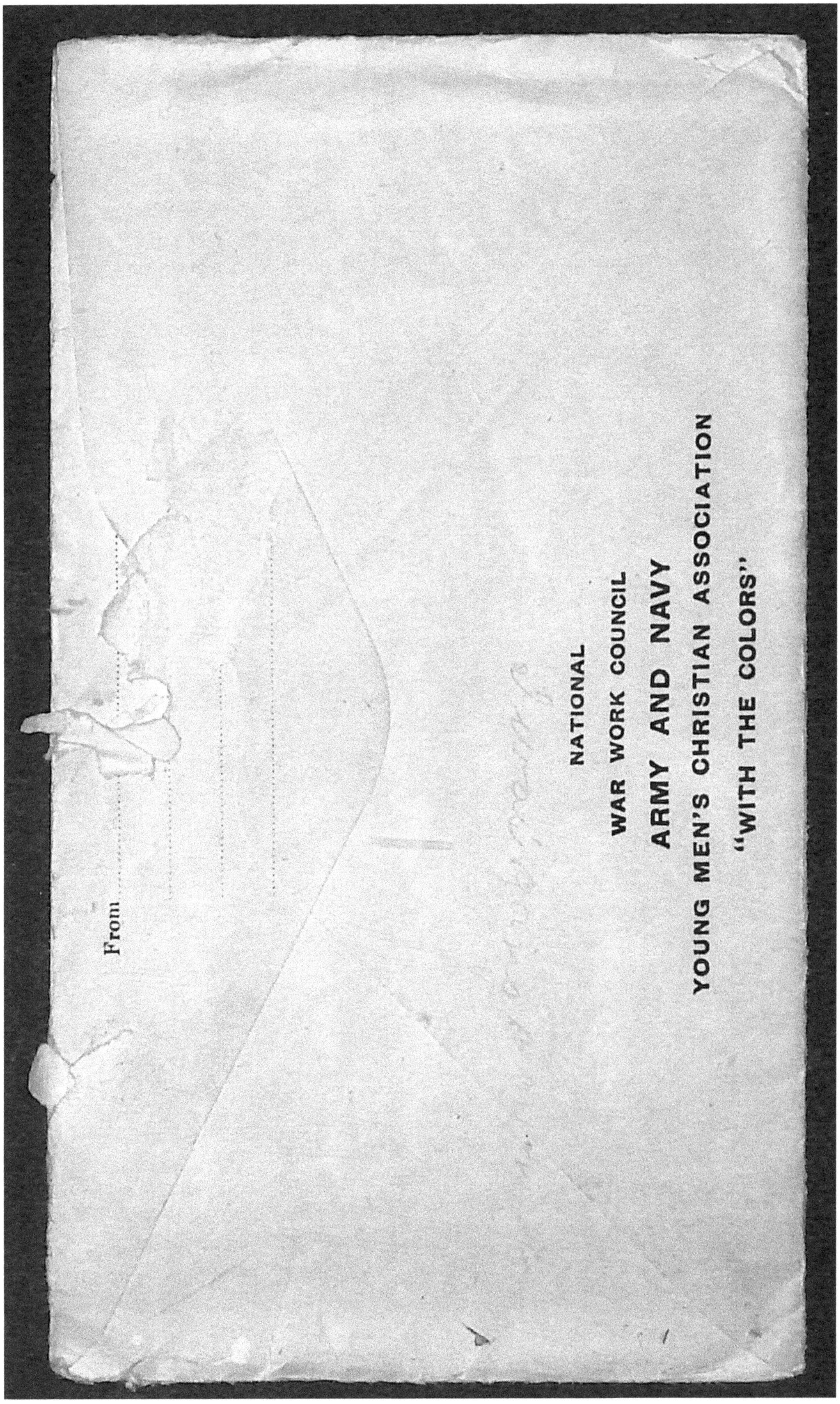
From
NATIONAL
WAR WORK COUNCIL
ARMY AND NAVY
YOUNG MEN'S CHRISTIAN ASSOCIATION
"WITH THE COLORS"

YMCA Letter Nov 2

408 Motor Supply Train Co 2G?

A E F New York.

Fellow ship mates

Friends from U of M

in Minnesota Group

took walk 10 miles

Green Hedges +

Stonewalls with broken glass

By a Bay

Had Canteen to buy

Censors Candy, wine etc

NO ~~DATE~~

FEB. 1 1918

Letter
No 2,

NATIONAL WAR WORK COUNCIL

YOUNG MEN'S CHRISTIAN ASSOCIATIONS

OF THE UNITED STATES

"WITH THE COLORS"

408th Motor Supply Train, Co. #369

A.E.F. via New York.

Friday.

Dear Mother,

There seems to be nothing of interest that I can write to you so I must write a little incidents that happen through the day.

I believe I forgot to tell you in my last letter that I met a fellow on the ship who used to be a good friend of Tom Johnson's and a Psi U pledge at the U. of W. We were very much surprised to see each other so far from home. He is in an Evacuation Hospital Unit that was organized some place in Minnesota.

Yesterday we took a long hike of about eight or ten miles and saw quite a bit of this beautiful country. The roads are much different from ours in that they are bordered almost everywhere by green hedges

NATIONAL WAR WORK COUNCIL

YOUNG MEN'S CHRISTIAN ASSOCIATIONS

OF THE UNITED STATES

"WITH THE COLORS"

or stone walls topped with brown grass. The better farms are beautifully kept and the buildings grouped close together and surrounded by a high wall with an iron gateway. The trees are of peculiar shape, probably due to the fact that the branches are all trimmed of when they get to be of good size, making a tree with a heavy gnarled trunk and small branches. Quite a few of the trees are overgrown with green vines that make the trunk look like a mass of green leaves. Along the road at short intervals are wine shops and here and there a wine press that gives of an odour that gives one a yearning to taste the contents of the barrels that can be seen through the doorway.

We hiked out along the bay to a fort or coast defence emplacement where we halted to rest. From there

NATIONAL WAR WORK COUNCIL
YOUNG MEN'S CHRISTIAN ASSOCIATIONS
OF THE UNITED STATES
"WITH THE COLORS"

we had quite a view of the surrounding country and the bay. We had quite a lot of fun trying to talk to the guards, who wanted to sell us a full rigged ship built inside of a bottle for the small sum of twenty francs. These Frenchmen are surely after our money - and are getting it.

I'm feeling fine, being fed unusually well and have a good warm bed so don't worry about me, for I am enjoying roughing it this way as long as I have the good friends that I have in our organization. I have made a fine new friend in Norman Martin, a Culver and Penn. State man from Beaver Pa., and sergeant drill master in #368 Co. He is a young married man and steady, so he is altogether a good friend to have.

NATIONAL WAR WORK COUNCIL

YOUNG MEN'S CHRISTIAN ASSOCIATIONS

OF THE UNITED STATES

"WITH THE COLORS"

The Y. M. C. A. here is doing good work in furnishing entertainments, in getting boys together to enjoy wholesome pleasures and sports, and in providing a reading and writing rooms and a canteen to buy tobacco, candy, and necessary toilet articles at. Mr West is not on the staff here so I must enquire and see if I can locate him. All my love to you all,

Affectionately,

Bob.

OK Lieut James Mulholland
U S 7408

POSTAL SERVICE
8 PM
1918

No 1

NATIONAL WAR WORK COUNCIL

YOUNG MEN'S CHRISTIAN ASSOCIATIONS

OF THE UNITED STATES

"WITH THE COLORS"

Dear Mother,

At last I have realized my great [illegible] to [illegible] service in France. We [illegible] three days [illegible] the deck [illegible] and [illegible] yesterday afternoon [illegible] with [illegible] on our backs.

What impressed me most when I [illegible] was the quaintness of the architecture. Nearly everything is either [illegible] or [illegible] composition of some kind or other and of a type that I have seen [illegible]. The [illegible] ville looks [illegible] some [illegible] setting or curtain that one may see in any of our theatres. Some of the lower class [illegible] are quite

NATIONAL WAR WORK COUNCIL

YOUNG MEN'S CHRISTIAN ASSOCIATIONS

OF THE UNITED STATES

"WITH THE COLORS"

---

picturesque costumes - I should say clothes - but most of them wear clothes very similar to ours.

France is a beautiful country as much as I have seen of it, and I wouldn't mind living there. The grass is already green and there are a lot of ornamental trees and shrubs which gives the country quite a striking appearance. The weather here is fine - [illegible] that it is rare - and the expression [illegible] sunny France certainly fits. It is so warm that I have been running around all day in my shirt.

The [illegible] girls and women are rouged quite a bit, but altogether are dirty in appearance

NATIONAL WAR WORK COUNCIL

YOUNG MEN'S CHRISTIAN ASSOCIATIONS

OF THE UNITED STATES

"WITH THE COLORS"

The other cities are pretty, not much harmed, but so disfigured. Something that made quite an impression was seeing most of the women on bicycles, a thing we seldom see at home anymore.

I wonder if the censor will object if I say that we expect to move toward the front tomorrow. It seems to me that that is not very vital information for an alien enemy, but you might like to consider to know where I am in a general way. So far I haven't seen anyone I know, but I hope to as I move on.

Well, dear mother, I must leave you to go to mess. Love to each and all of you at home.

Affectionately,

OK James Mulholland Med Rt Your Bob.

2 M C U A M S J 408

FEB 23, 1918
2 POST CARDS TO SADIE
received Jan. 8 letter
got 5 WI STATE JOURNALS
letter from Aunt. Belle
"TRESORET POSTES" IN FRANCE
?/20/18

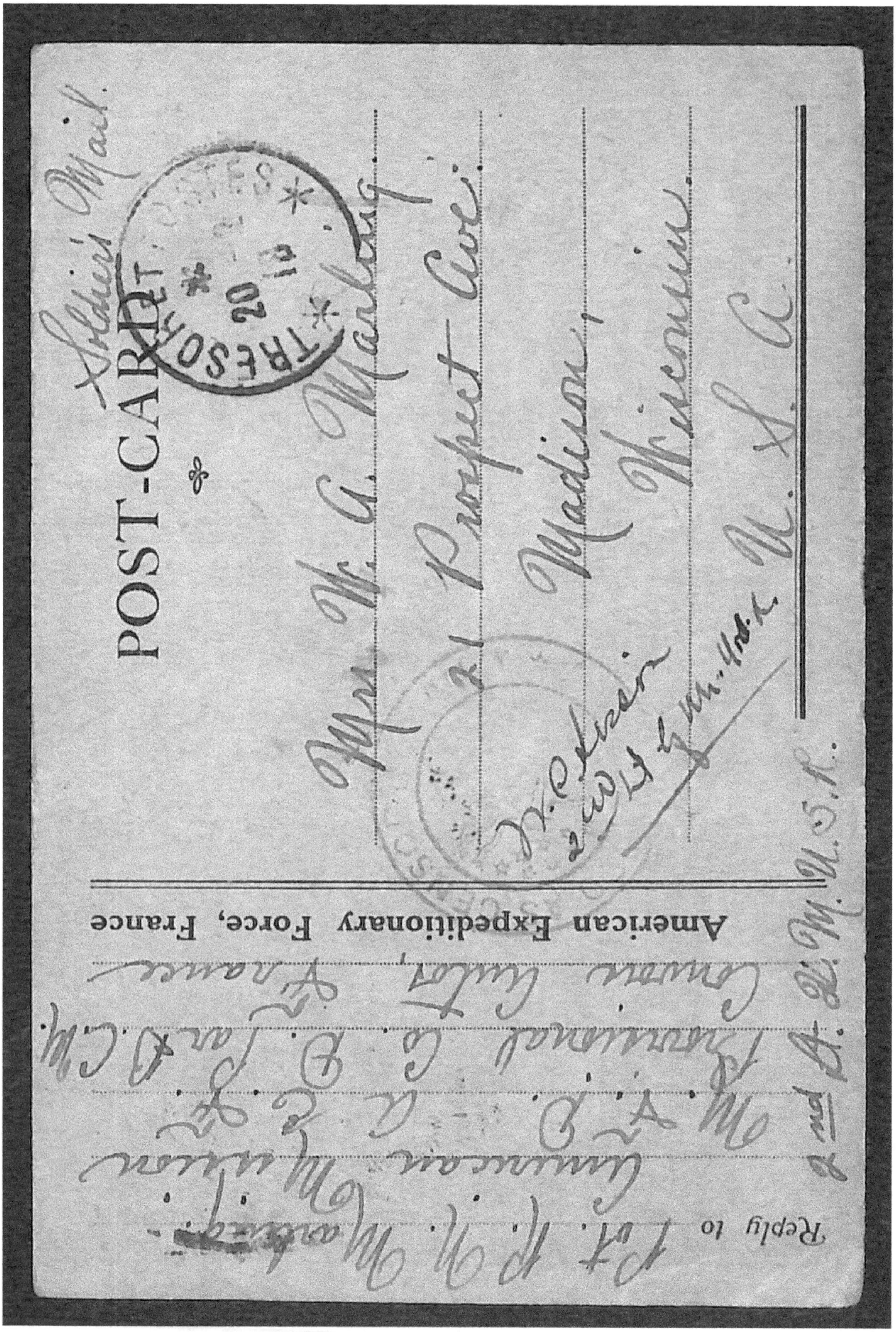
POST-CARD
Soldiers' Mail
Mrs W. A.
21 Prospect Ave.
Madison,
Wisconsin
U. S. A.
American Expeditionary Force, France
Reply to

POST-CARD
Soldier's Mail
TRESOR ET POSTES
10-22
18
A.E.F. PASSED AS CENSORED
American Expeditionary Force, France
Reply to
A.E.F.
New York

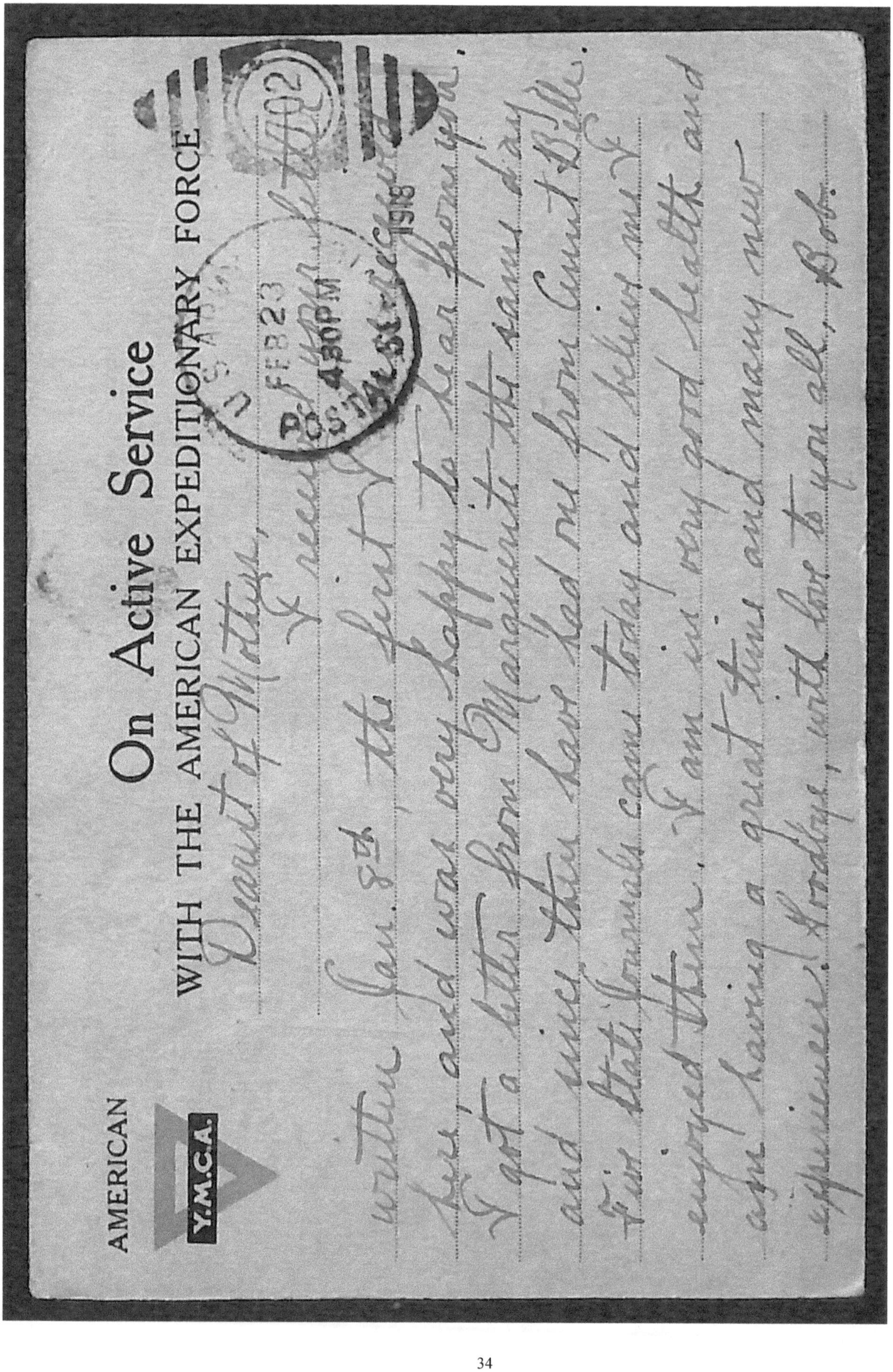
AMERICAN

Y.M.C.A.

On Active Service

WITH THE AMERICAN EXPEDITIONARY FORCE

FEB 23

4 30 PM

1918

Dearest of Mothers,

I received your letter written Jan. 8th, the first I received here, and was very happy to hear from you. I got a letter from Marguerite the same day and since then have had one from Aunt Belle. Five State Journals came today and believe me I enjoyed them. I am in very good health and am having a great time and many new experiences. Goodbye, with love to you all, Bob.

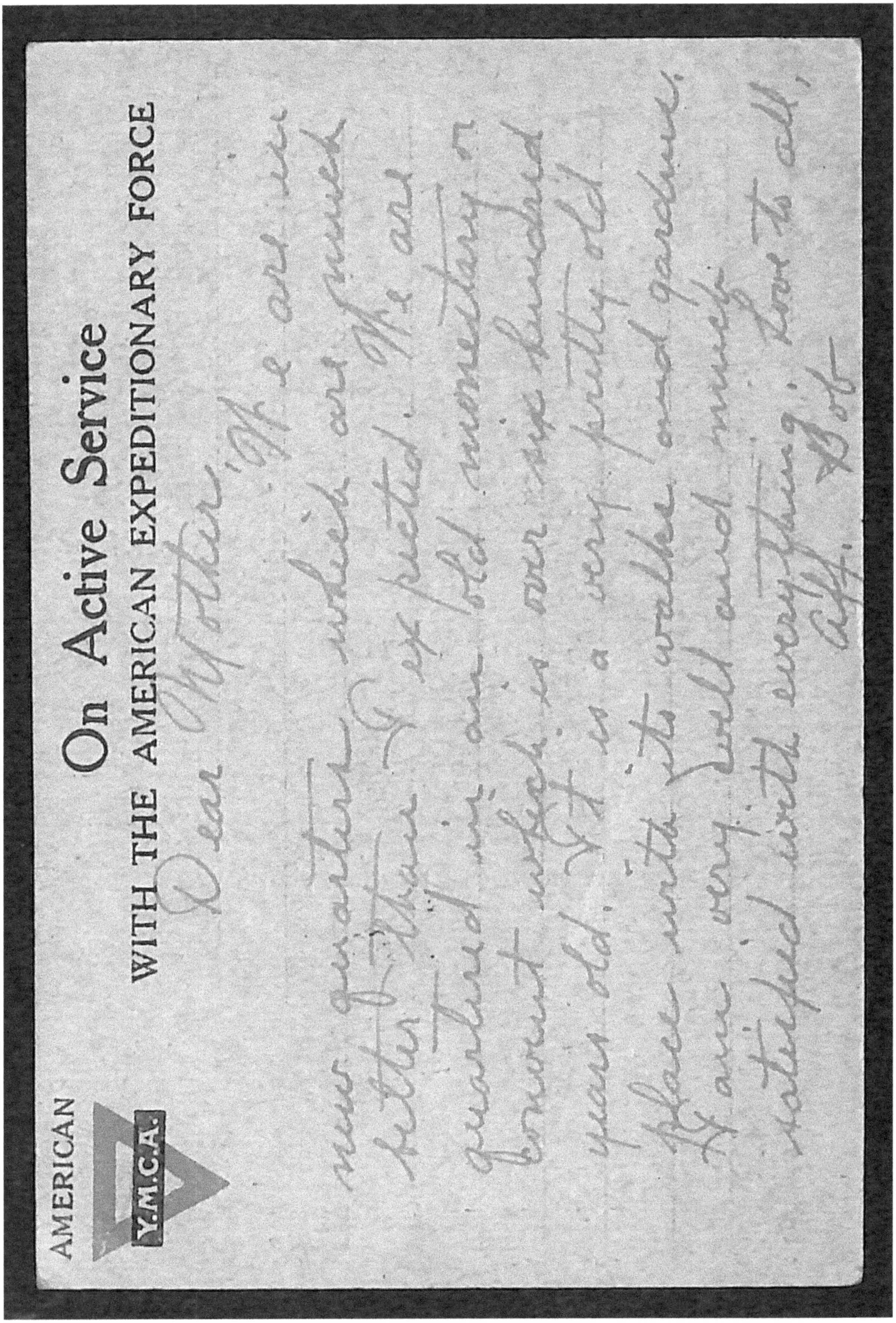

AMERICAN
Y.M.C.A.
On Active Service
WITH THE AMERICAN EXPEDITIONARY FORCE

Dear Mother,
We are in new quarters which are much better than I expected. We are quartered in an old monestary or convent which is over six hundred years old. It is a very pretty old place with its walks and gardens. I am very well and much satisfied with everything. Love to all,
Aff. Bob

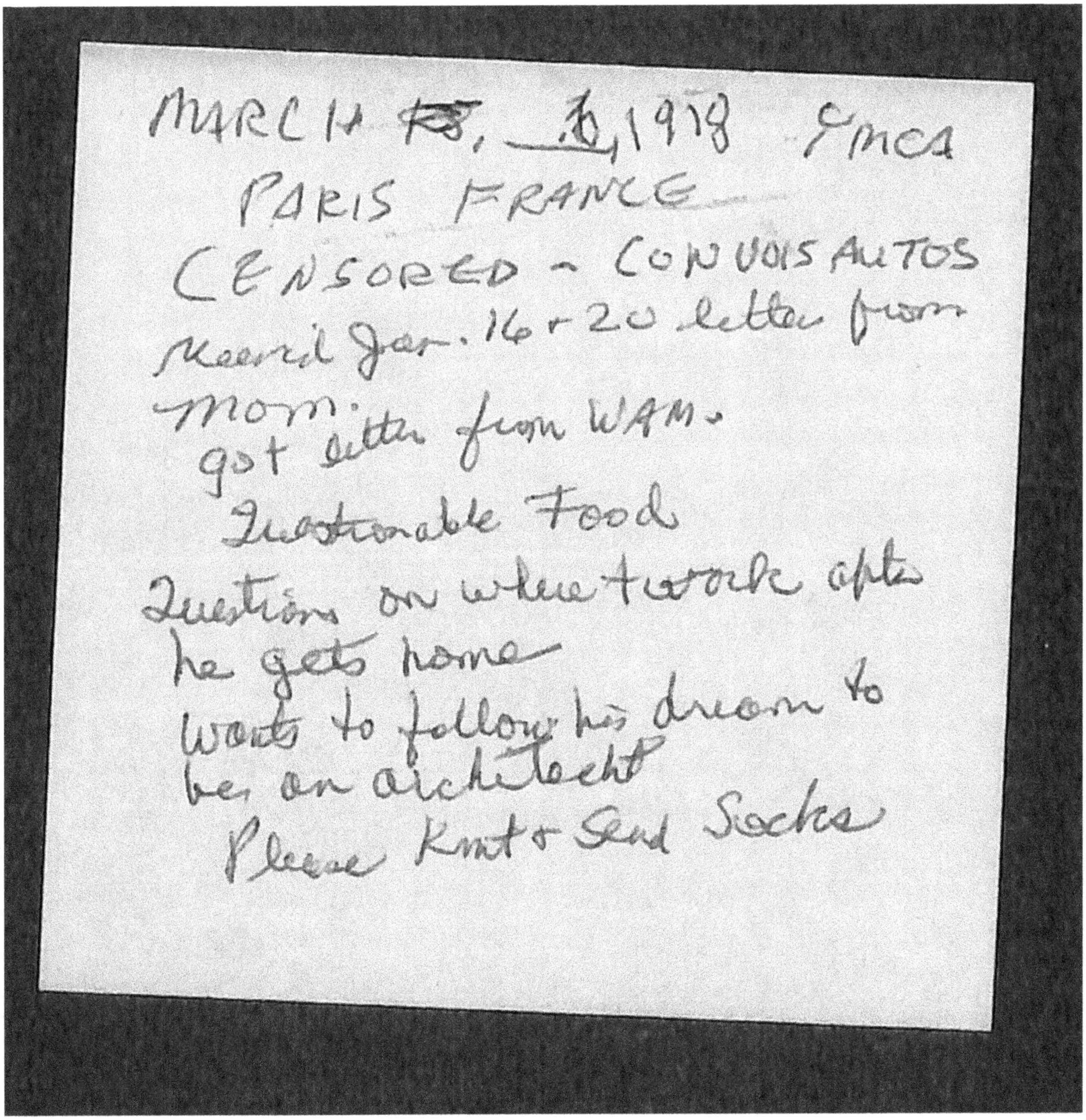
MARCH ~~15~~, 16, 1918 YMCA
PARIS FRANCE
CENSORED - CONVOIS AUTOS
Received Jan. 16 + 20 letter from
mom.
got letter from WAM.
Questionable Food
Questions on where to work after
he gets home
Wants to follow his dream to
be an architect
Please Knit & Send Socks

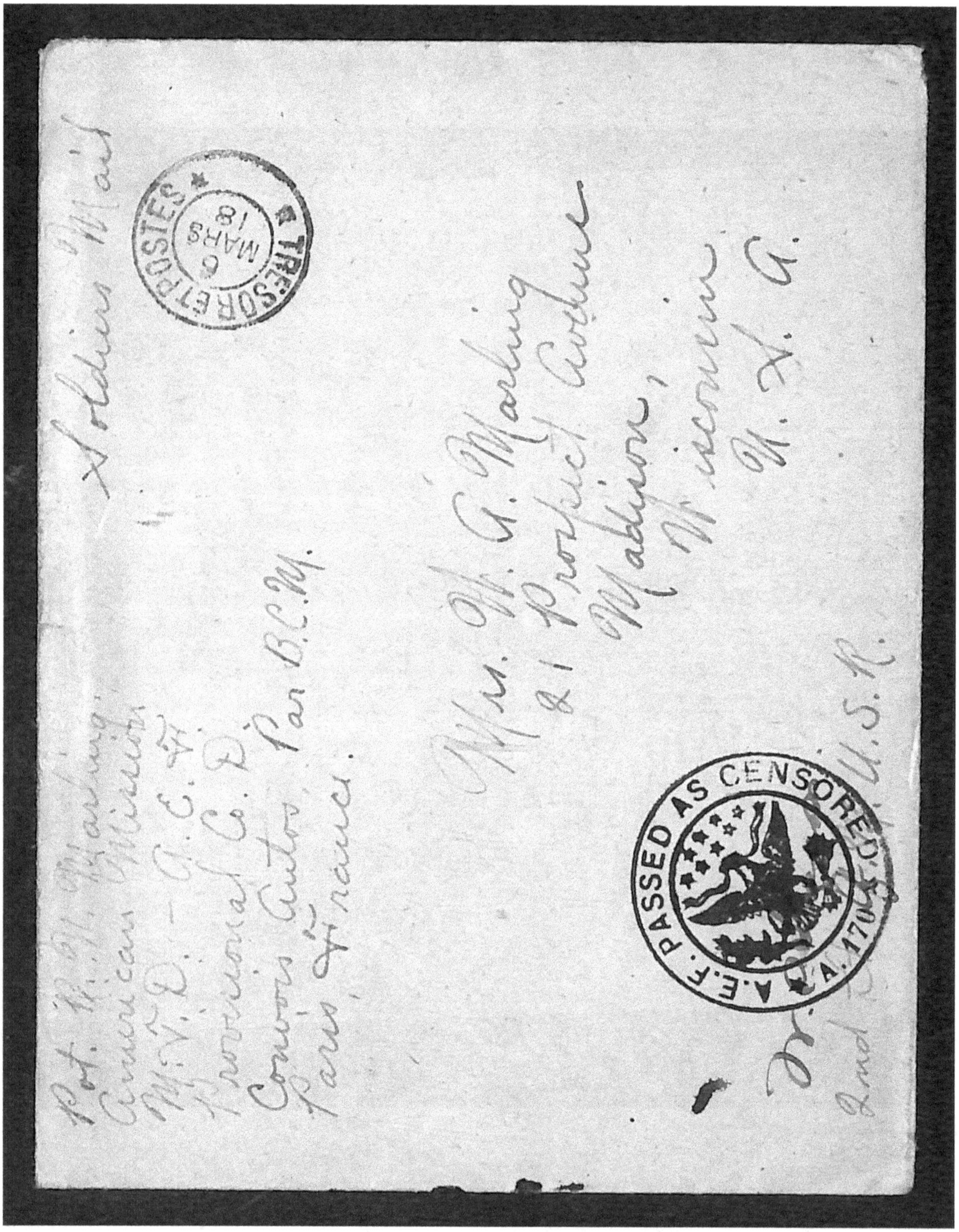
Soldiers Mail
TRESOR ET POSTES
6 MARS 18
Madison,
Wisconsin
U.S.A.
A.E.F. PASSED AS CENSORED

Pvt. H. L. Maring
American Mission
M. T. D. - A. E. F.
Provisional Co. D.
Par B. C. M.
Convois Autos
Paris, France.

AMERICAN Y.M.C.A.

ON ACTIVE SERVICE
WITH THE
AMERICAN EXPEDITIONARY FORCE

.... 191

Mother Dearest,

The last time I received mail from home I got your letter of January 16th and the other of January 20th. I haven't had a great deal of time lately to write by managed to get one off to Father and another that I had been owing to Marguerite for about two weeks. Just now I'm about eight letters behind and will have to do some tall hustling to catch up as I can't write more than two or three letters an evening. Today I received a letter from Dad dated Feb 1st and also letters from Howard Sherman and Elizabeth. All of them were very interesting. Father told me in

AMERICAN Y.M.C.A.

ON ACTIVE SERVICE
WITH THE
AMERICAN EXPEDITIONARY FORCE

191

his letter that your leg was still giving you trouble. I hope that by the time you get this, it will be all healed.

Father seems to think that Bill is pretty apt to join me this summer. His best chance would be to try for a commission, and I know he is competent to hold one. If he should try this army fare for a while I'm afraid that his stomach would be as bad or worse than it ever has been. Not that I'm kicking on our food here but I have eaten some very questionable compounds concocted by some of our army "cooks". Here in Company D we are blessed by

AMERICAN Y.M.C.A.

ON ACTIVE SERVICE
WITH THE
AMERICAN EXPEDITIONARY FORCE

....191

a real cook who can make things "just like mother used to".

I suppose that I should forget (for the present) about what to do when I return but I can't help feeling the desire to go back to college. I would like to go in with father for the sake of closer companionship, but I really don't take much to the lumber business and would like to follow up my dream of being an architect. But remains to be seen whether or not I will have any capacity for study when I get back. Army life or that of a private isn't liable to give rise to elevating thots and ambitions. The highest

AMERICAN
Y.M.C.A.

ON ACTIVE SERVICE
WITH THE
AMERICAN EXPEDITIONARY FORCE

__________ 191

level might be found I believe in Aviation and I believe I will again make a try for it. If I can't pass the physical for officers training I'd like to get into it as a private and work up.

You might start on some socks now for I surely will be in need of them by the time you have them made and sent to me. Don't forget to send me a carton of Omars or Fatimas every week or two because many of them stop short of their destination, so the fellows here tell me.

Love to you all
Bob.

NO DATE 3/22 + 3/25 YMCA
3/15/1918
Received - 2 Letters
VIEWS OF U of W
He sent transfer for aviation
Uncle Irv Business in trouble
France Business are suffering
Long Convoy 52 hours
with out sleep and slept in
Cannon No. 10 shoes later
30 or 40 mile gale + no lights
15 to 20 mph

Censored

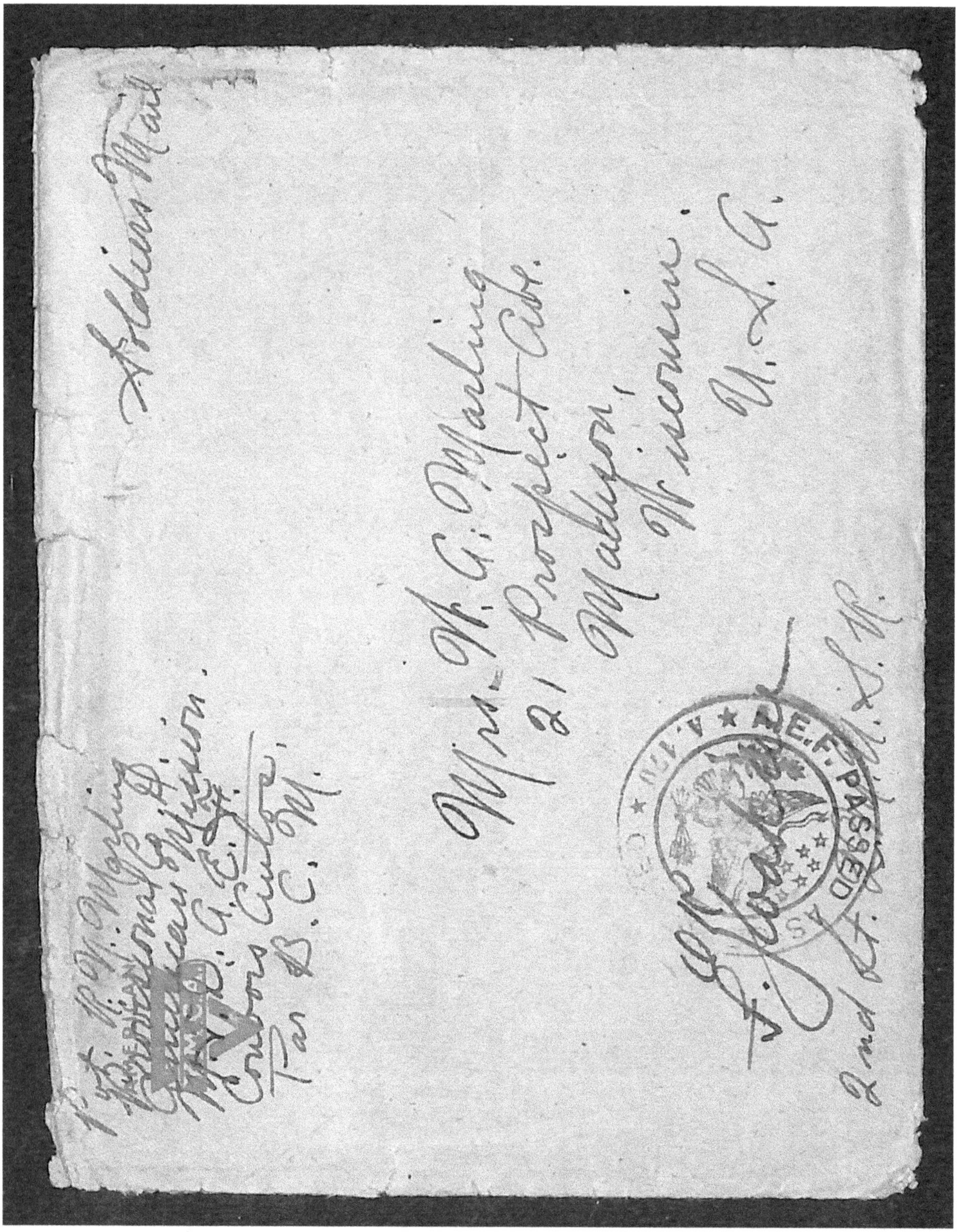
Soldiers Mail
Mrs. H. C. Marling
21 Prospect Ave.
Madison,
Wisconsin,
U.S.A.
A.E.F. PASSED

Pvt. R. Y. Marling
Prov. Co. D
American Mission
M. D. A. E. F.
Construction
Par C. M.

ON ACTIVE SERVICE
WITH THE
AMERICAN EXPEDITIONARY FORCE

__________191__

Dear Mother,

The other day I received two letters from you, one dated Mar. 22 & one Mar. 25, and today I received your letter of March 15th. I'll answer them according to date.

I was very much pleased to get the views of the U. of W., for being a Wisconsin man I've naturally praised her to the skies. Now I have something to show the fellows to back my boast that there are no state universities in the U. S. that can surpass it. Of course pictures can prove a great deal but they can show the beauties of the place. I had a little pang of home-sickness when I first opened the folder and saw all the familiar buildings and the associations they brought back to me. It set me to wondering if I would ever return again as a student and if I would return at all.

I don't want to worry you but I must deceive you, so must tell you that my transfer is in for aviation. I feel, even more than ever, that I must get into that field. You speak of the many accidents and deaths at the camps in the States. I have it from pretty reliable sources that the machines were

has been such a long time
since I last heard of him.
He seems to be on the outs
with me. Both he and his
mother have neglected to
answer letters I sent them
before I entered the army.
I dont take much stock
in either of them. They are
too self-satisfied.

Very sorry to hear of
Uncle Trov's. reverses. Business
seems to be knocked out
completely. Still the States
dont know what hard times
mean. You ought to see
poor France. Nearly all
business is dead. Just a
few shops and cafe's and
restraunts open. I'm speaking

AMERICAN Y.M.C.A.

ON ACTIVE SERVICE
WITH THE
AMERICAN EXPEDITIONARY FORCE

________________191__

defectice due to German
agents' work in the factories.
Over here we will not have
that to contend with. Still
there are dangers enough, I
know, and if I should "go
West" in such a service I
will have no regret except
for the sorrow it will cause
you. And I know that you
will not oppose me in this,
for I feel its my duty and
priviledge to make the best
use of my life. I would far
rather live but a year or two
doing something worth while,
than many years filled with
mediocrity.

I was very much interested
in hearing about Lander. It

AMERICAN Y.M.C.A.

ON ACTIVE SERVICE
WITH THE
AMERICAN EXPEDITIONARY FORCE

_____________ 191_

only of cities or towns in the zone of the advance or war-zone.

Just a few days ago we were out on a long convoy. We were gone for about fifty-two hours without sleep and before I went to bed in Camion No. 10 it had been sixty some hours since my last real sleep. I slept now and then on the truck. Imagine riding over rough roads on a five-ton truck and being so tired that you can sleep sitting up. Not only sleeping sitting up but ~~but~~ sleeping and driving the truck. Of course the sleep was short at the wheel for the car would soon be off the road ~~and~~ I would open my eyes with a start and get back again on the road. The worst of it was driving without lights. Not that we could not have them on, but it was impossible to light them in a thirty or forty mile gale. So I had to follow the truck ahead and steer by his tail light and "feel" the road running at a rate of fifteen to twenty miles an hour most of the time. Many times my heart was up in my mouth as I just missed something or other or when I imagined I saw a camion, cow, man, or wall dead ahead of me. It was nervous work believe me.

Goodbye with love to you all.

Your aff. son,

Bob. BPW

YMCA - MARCH 17, 1918

Answer to letter 2/15/18
Need to write Uncle IRV &
Aunt Amy — thank for Candy.
Wants to put in application
for aviation.
Needs. 6 sets BVD's & toilet
kit items.
Has heard a few shells &
Bursts.

Censored

AMERICAN
YMCA
PASSED AS CENSORED
A.E.F.
A. 170

Pvt. R. N. Marling.
American Mission
Provisional Co. D.
M. T. D. - A. E. F.
Convois Autos
Par B. C. M.

In answer to letter of Feb. 15th.

AMERICAN Y.M.C.A.

ON ACTIVE SERVICE
WITH THE
AMERICAN EXPEDITIONARY FORCE

March 17 1918

Dear Mother,

Your welcome letters have been arriving pretty regularly lately, the latest one dated February 18th and that received yesterday or the day before. That is not bad time at all, is it? But I suppose I will receive some written at an earlier date a few days from now.

Your writing about Uncle Fro. and Aunt Amy makes me think that I will have to write to them soon and thank them for the Keeley's Candies that I received just the other day. They were fine and a very pleasant change after eating French and

AMERICAN
Y.M.C.A.

ON ACTIVE SERVICE
WITH THE
AMERICAN EXPEDITIONARY FORCE

..........................191

Swiss candy for so long.
I'm very glad to hear that you are up and about again, and I hope that your leg gives you no more trouble. Let us hope that the bone isn't injured.
The sinking of the Tuscania was rather a blessing in a way. It woke people at home to the fact that we are really in this war in a vital sense. Kind of made people start thinking and those who could, to enlisting for active service. Even I do not feel that I am giving the best there is in me. I am going to put in an

AMERICAN Y.M.C.A.

ON ACTIVE SERVICE
WITH THE
AMERICAN EXPEDITIONARY FORCE

191

application for aviation right away and I hope that I will be fortunate enough to have it accepted. You probably have heard that Bill and Jack Robson are already in training in Texas and must be flying by this time.

If you will please, I wish you would send my toilet set and replace those articles that I have already taken from it. I would also be much pleased with six suits of B.V.Ds, and if I am still here in France next Fall please send on my heavies for I much prefer them to army issue.

AMERICAN Y.M.C.A.

ON ACTIVE SERVICE
WITH THE
AMERICAN EXPEDITIONARY FORCE

.... 191

The weather is fine here, although the nights are still rather cold. Just ideal for B.V.D.s. I have been wearing a suit given to me by one of the Field Service men for about a week, and find it just right.

Lately I have been having a few new experiences and am seeing new sights. I have heard big shells shriek and burst etc., and seen an exciting air battle or two and a couple boche planes dropped.

Love to you all,

Affectionately,

Bob.

O.K.
F.J.W.

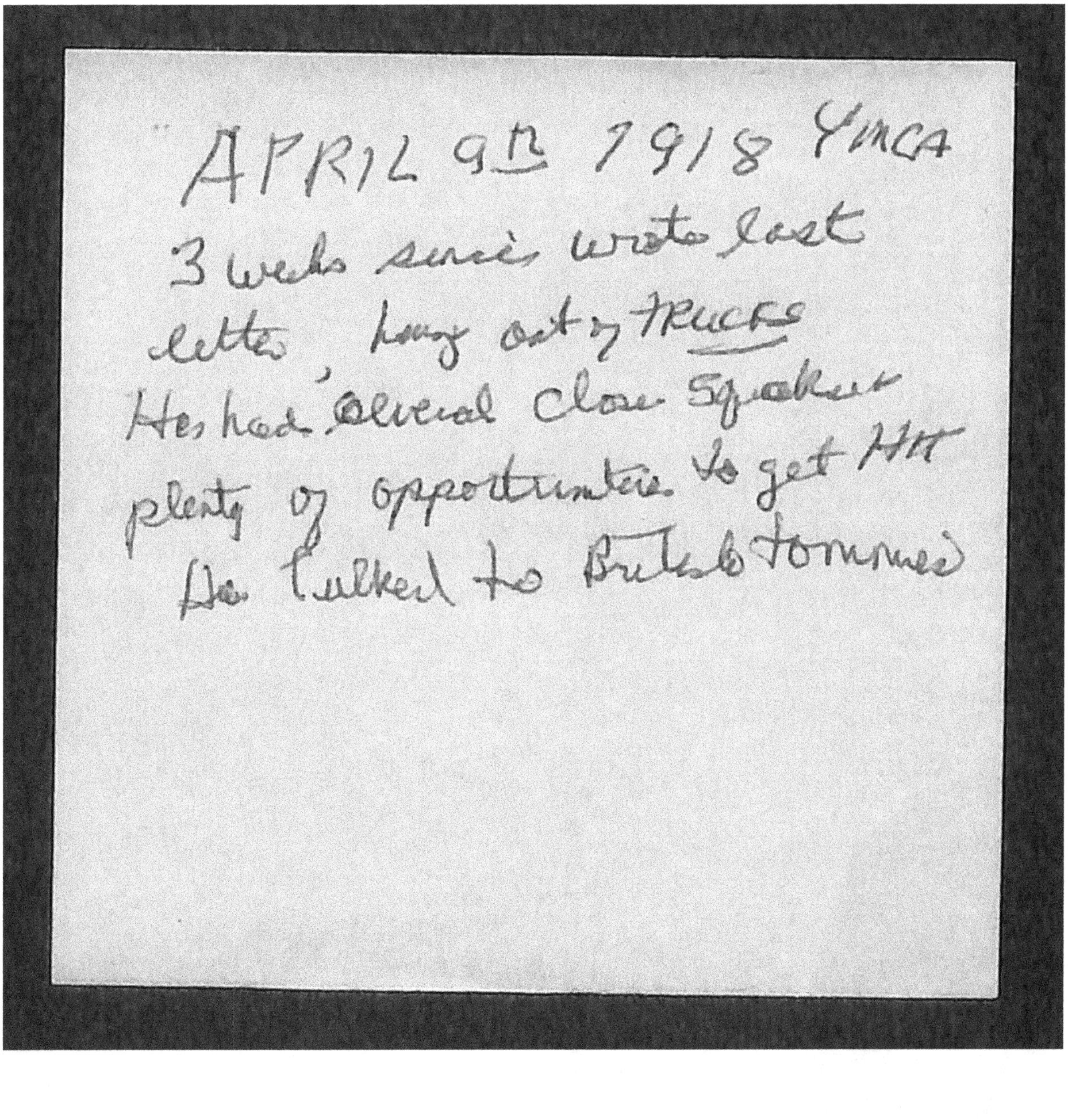

APRIL 9th 1918 YMCA

3 weeks since wrote last letter, being out of TRUCKS

He's had several close squeaks

plenty of opportunities to get Hit

Has talked to British Tommies

AMERICAN Y.M.C.A.

ON ACTIVE SERVICE
WITH THE
AMERICAN EXPEDITIONARY FORCE

April 9th 1918

Dear Mother,

I have received several letters from you since I last wrote to you. For the past two weeks or so we have been very busy and very unsettled, living like gipsies along the road, sleeping in our camions etc. I have not had many opportunities to write and had no paper to write on. And so day by day slipped by and I still put off writing until now it must be about three weeks since I got off my last letter. I'll try to do better after this for I know you must worry if you do not hear from me more often than that.

I have had several close squeaks and plenty of opportunities to get hit but it seems that a lucky streak will pull one through a tight place. We are now as you already know are having one of the wars greatest and bloodiest battles. That is bloody for the boche. This is the time when our organization comes in for hard work with long hours. The work hasn't been very hard so far but you never know when you may be called upon to test your powers of endurance.

AMERICAN Y.M.C.A.

ON ACTIVE SERVICE
WITH THE
AMERICAN EXPEDITIONARY FORCE

______________ 191__

Your latest letter, that of March 17th, reached me two or three days ago. I was very glad to hear that the Wisconsin boys are safely over here, and would like very much to run across some of them for I've only seen two, that I knew in the States, since I've been over here. One was Harold Kelly at a port north of Bordeaux, and the other is Fritz Legler who is driving a staff car for Major Robinson of the American Mission. But even though our fellows are now here in France, I hardly expect to see them, for I am with the French and scarcely ever see Americans except those in truck companies. I've seen and talked with the British Tommies quite a bit and find them quite interesting to talk to. One has to keep his ears open to understand them for they speak English that is far different from that spoken in the States.

I started this letter yesterday but was called out to roll call right in the middle of a sentence. I was late at that, and consequently "held the sack" - got special detail that afternoon, and had to help clean up a stable yard. Then, after finishing that job, I had to make a trip in my camion - truck - and got back to camp too late to finish the letter, so I'm taking time now. Received a splendid letter from Ruth Johnson about three days ago. It seems that she too is getting pretty tired

AMERICAN Y.M.C.A.

ON ACTIVE SERVICE
WITH THE
AMERICAN EXPEDITIONARY FORCE

____________ 191__

of school with so many things pertaining to War are going on about her. I suppose that she will be wanting her father to let her do office work in his new Ordinance Factory.

The last I heard about Bill and the new draft is that he was about to sign up with the Home Guard. I suppose he will have to be satisfied with that for a while, but I hope he gets out of it later, it sounds so much like a four o'clock tea club to me.

It's mighty good of you all to write so often, and I hope you keep up the good work for a letter from home is a great help now and then. Tell Dad he's got a letter coming just as soon as I have time. Enclosed find paper that father sent to me to be signed. I am in very good health and having nothing to complain of. Love to you all,

Your aff. son,
Bob.

OK F.J.W.

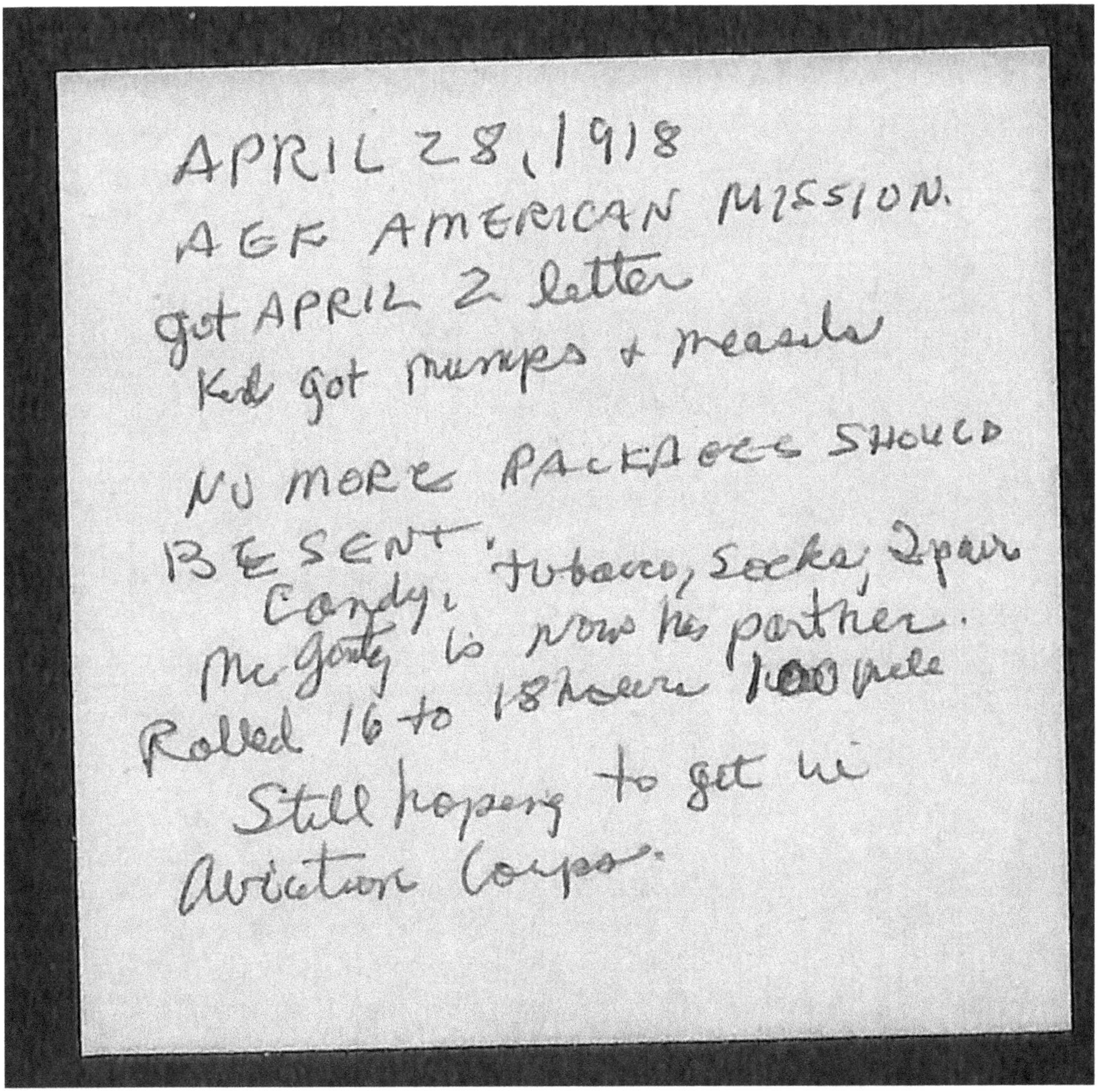
APRIL 28, 1918
AEF AMERICAN MISSION.
got APRIL 2 letter
Kid got mumps & measles
NO MORE PACKAGES SHOULD
BE SENT. Tobacco, Socks, 2 pair
Candy.
McGarty is now his partner.
Rolled 16 to 18 hours 100 mile
Still hoping to get in
Aviation Corps.

PASSED AS CENSORED

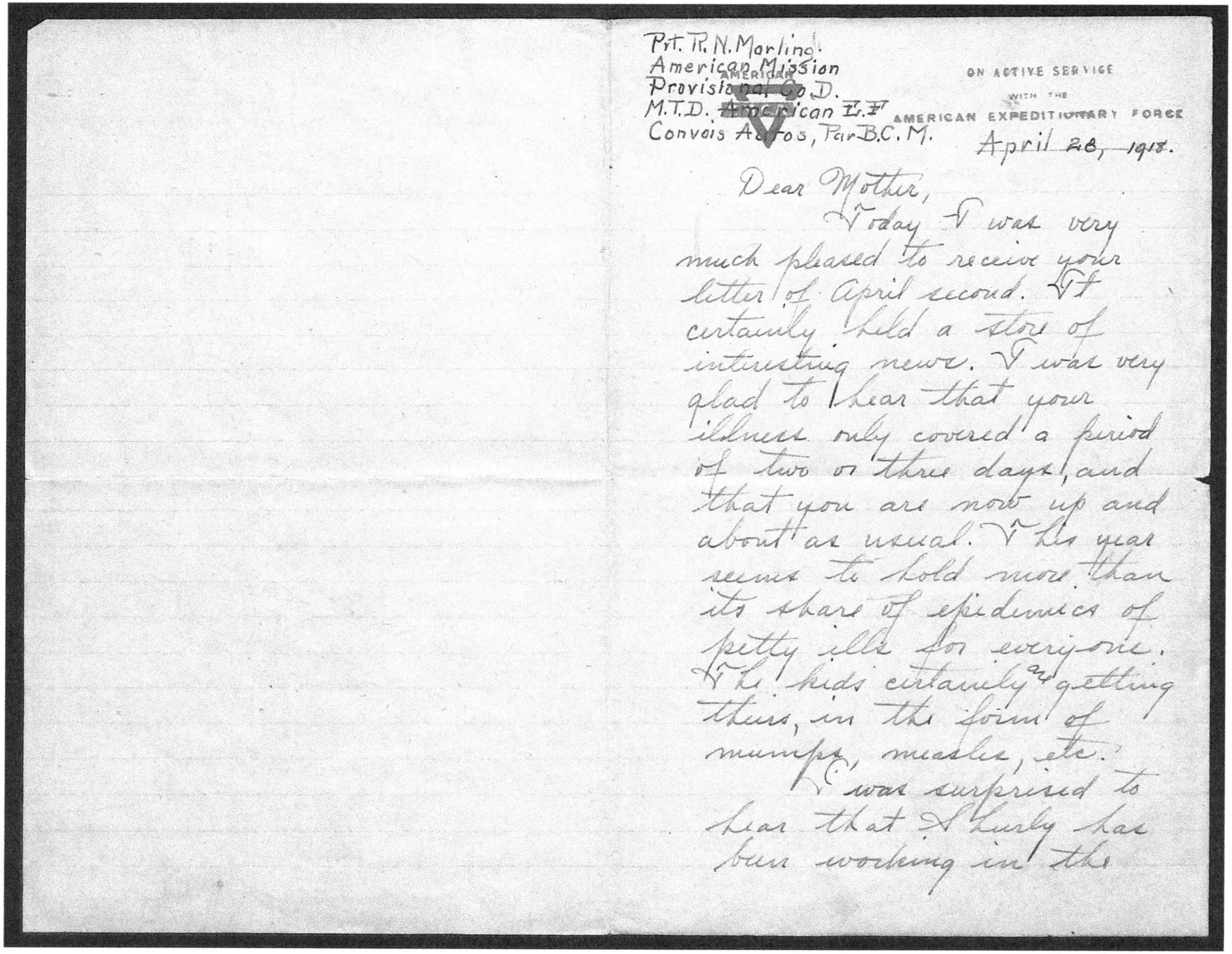

Pvt. R. N. Marling.
American Mission
Provisional Co. D.
M.T.D. ~~American~~ E.F.
Convois Autos, Par B.C.M.

ON ACTIVE SERVICE
WITH THE
AMERICAN EXPEDITIONARY FORCE

AMERICAN

April 28, 1918.

Dear Mother,

Today I was very much pleased to receive your letter of April second. It certainly held a store of interesting news. I was very glad to hear that your illness only covered a period of two or three days, and that you are now up and about as usual. This year seems to hold more than its share of epidemics of petty ills for every-one. The kids certainly are getting theirs, in the form of mumps, measles, etc.

I was surprised to hear that Shirley has been working in the

Forrest Products Labratory. The last letter I received from him, stated that he was about to enter the Navy in the radio department. I wonder if his plans have fallen through, or if he is just waiting for the radio school in Chicago to open.

I heard from Ruth again the other day, and she told me of Cootes death, and how much they missed him. She also said that her father was then in the East and that he would try to find another dog to take Cootes place. I don't believe that they can find another as intelligent and as full of life, or as nearly human

AMERICAN Y.M.C.A.

ON ACTIVE SERVICE
WITH THE
AMERICAN EXPEDITIONARY FORCE

as he was. What have you done with Scout? Sent him up to William as you had intended to do?

Yes, packages are not to be sent unless by request, and that request signed (O.K.) by my C.O. That means the loss of such comforts as candy and cigarettes. That reminds me, - your packages of Candy, tobacco, and sox - two pair - have come and are giving me pleasure. The tobacco was spilled a bit, and the can badly bent, but otherwise everthing was in fine shape. The candy is very nice, and McGinty (my "pardner") and

I enjoy a few pieces now and then.

The day before yesterday I was put on guard from 11 P.M. to 1 AM and then we rolled at 4:30. We made a pretty long trip, of more than a hundred miles and got back at about 11 o'clock last night. The country is now very beautiful, after frequent rains, and I enjoyed every bit of the trip. I saw several chateaus, some quite modern and beautiful, others ancient and in ruins. You used to be so tired and stiff after a four to eight hour run in the car, and I used to think it quite a jaunt. How would you feel after a eighteen to twenty

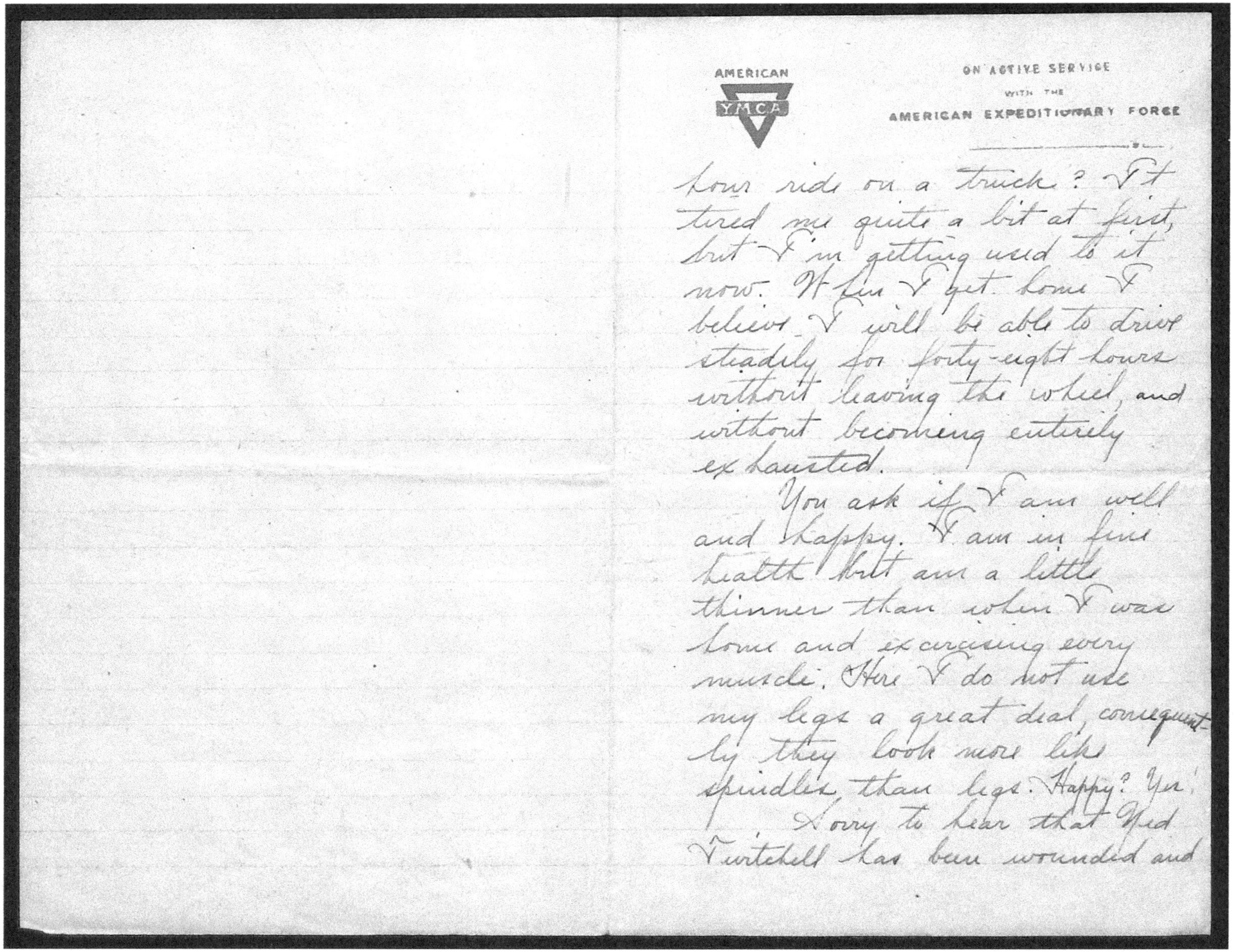

AMERICAN
YMCA
ON ACTIVE SERVICE
WITH THE
AMERICAN EXPEDITIONARY FORCE

hour ride on a truck? It tired me quite a bit at first, but I'm getting used to it now. When I get home I believe I will be able to drive steadily for forty-eight hours without leaving the wheel, and without becoming entirely exhausted.

You ask if I am well and happy. I am in fine health but am a little thinner than when I was home and exercising every muscle. Here I do not use my legs a great deal, consequently they look more like spindles than legs. Happy? Yes!

Sorry to hear that Ned Twitchell has been wounded and

that Dud Davis — I suppose I
should say Lt. Davis — has
had such a bad fall. By the way,
what service is Ned in, and
what is his rank? I didn't
know that he had come over,
or that he was even in the
army. Glad to hear that
Jimmy Vincent is now a
First Lieut. With so many
of the old Phi Delts rising
so rapidly, it will not be
hard to get recommendations
from officers when the time
comes for me to ask for
them: For if my application
for aviation goes through,
and I hope it does, I will
need a few O.K's. to help
me realize my ambitions.
With so many, in fact nearly
all, of my friends sporting bars

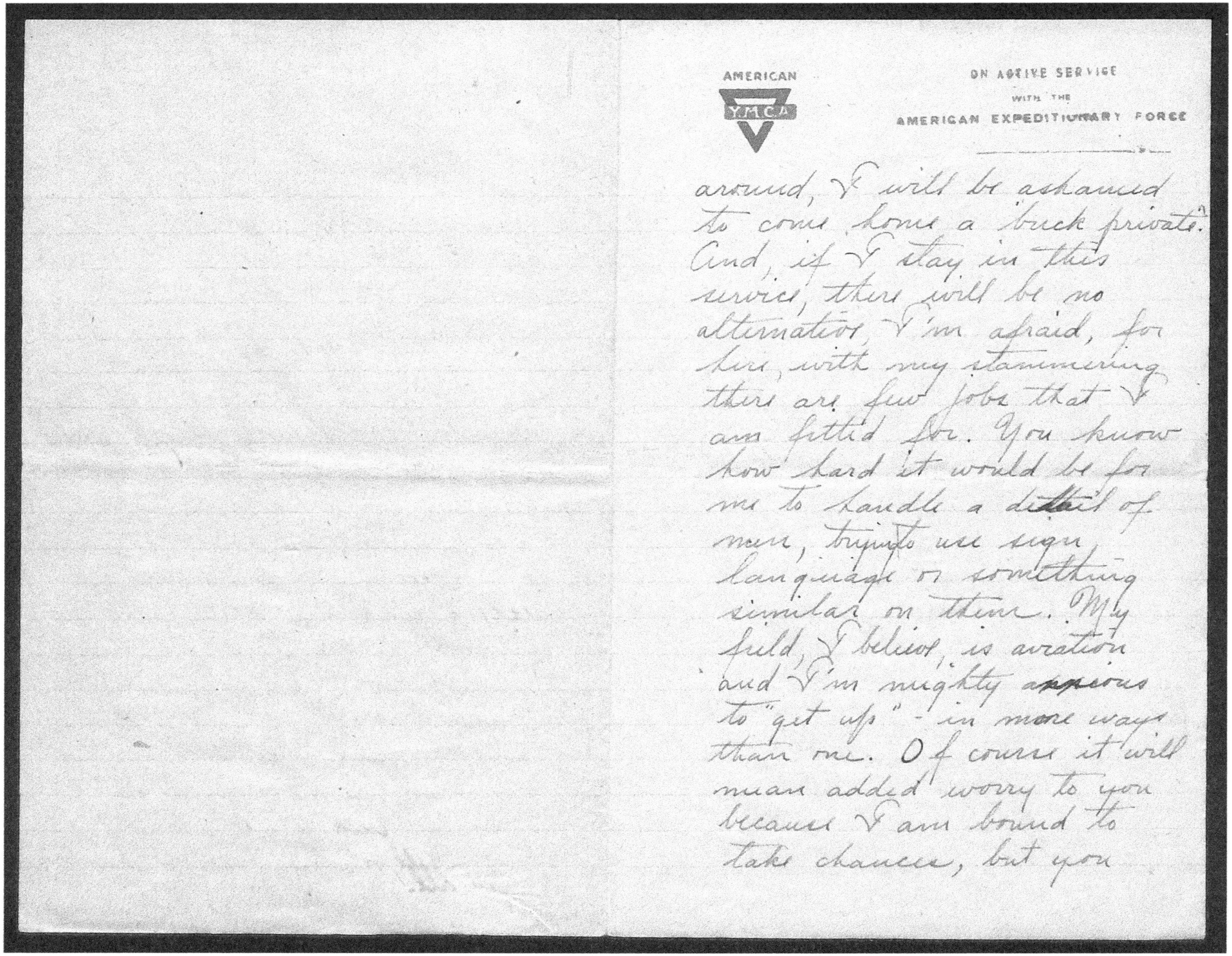
AMERICAN Y.M.C.A.

ON ACTIVE SERVICE WITH THE AMERICAN EXPEDITIONARY FORCE

around, I will be ashamed
to come home a "buck private."
And, if I stay in this
service, there will be no
alternative, I'm afraid, for
here, with my stammering
there are few jobs that I
am fitted for. You know
how hard it would be for
me to handle a detail of
men, trying to use sign
language or something
similar on them. My
field, I believe, is aviation
and I'm mighty anxious
to "get up" - in more ways
than one. Of course it will
mean added worry to you
because I am bound to
take chances, but you

have never known me to refuse to take a chance. I guess it must be in my blood, for I can't stand this slow service, with so little excitement, and such comparative safety. I want to be doing something and I will do something provided things break my way.

As it is I will have to go into aviation as a private and depend upon my personality to make enough friends to recommend me for the ground school, then things will come more easily. It has never been hard for me to make friends, and I believe that I will find them in the new service if I have the luck to get into it.

Well, my heart full of love for you all. Affectionately, Bob.

OK. J.J.W.

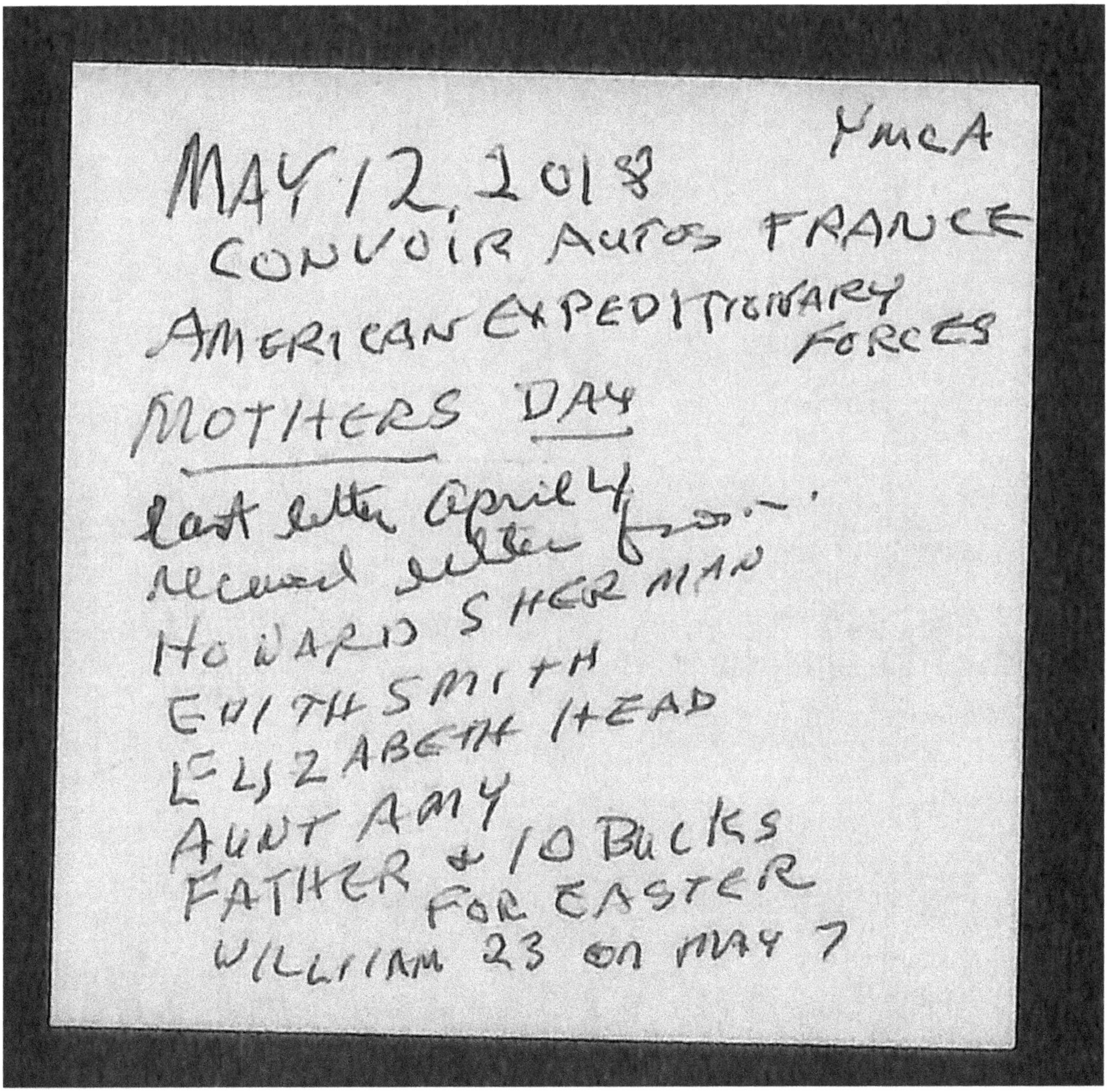
YMCA

MAY 12, 1918
CONVOIR AUTOS FRANCE
AMERICAN EXPEDITIONARY FORCES

MOTHERS DAY

last letter april 4
received letter from
HOWARD SHERMAN
EDITH SMITH
ELIZABETH HEAD
AUNT AMY
FATHER + 10 BUCKS FOR EASTER
WILLIAM 23 on MAY 7

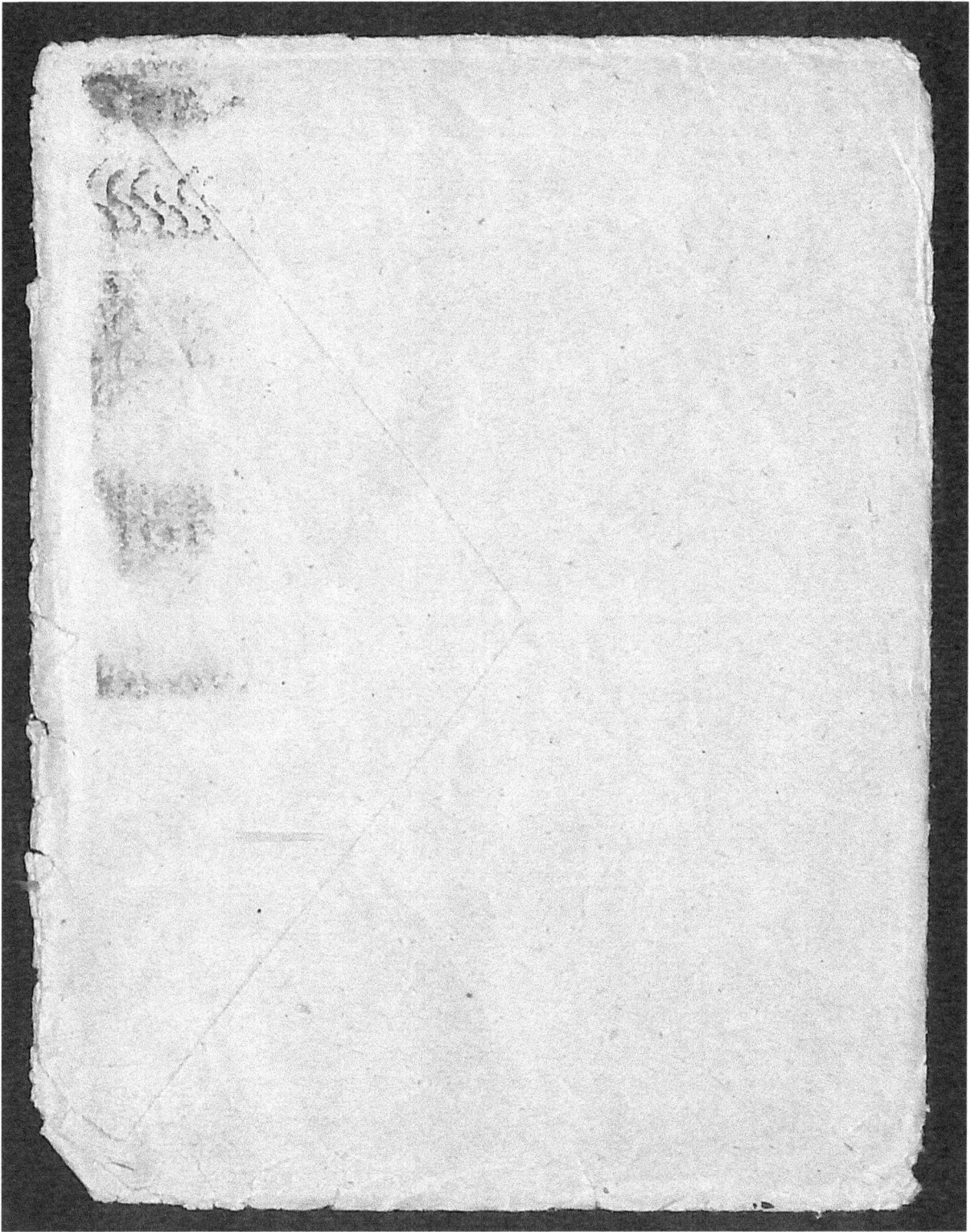

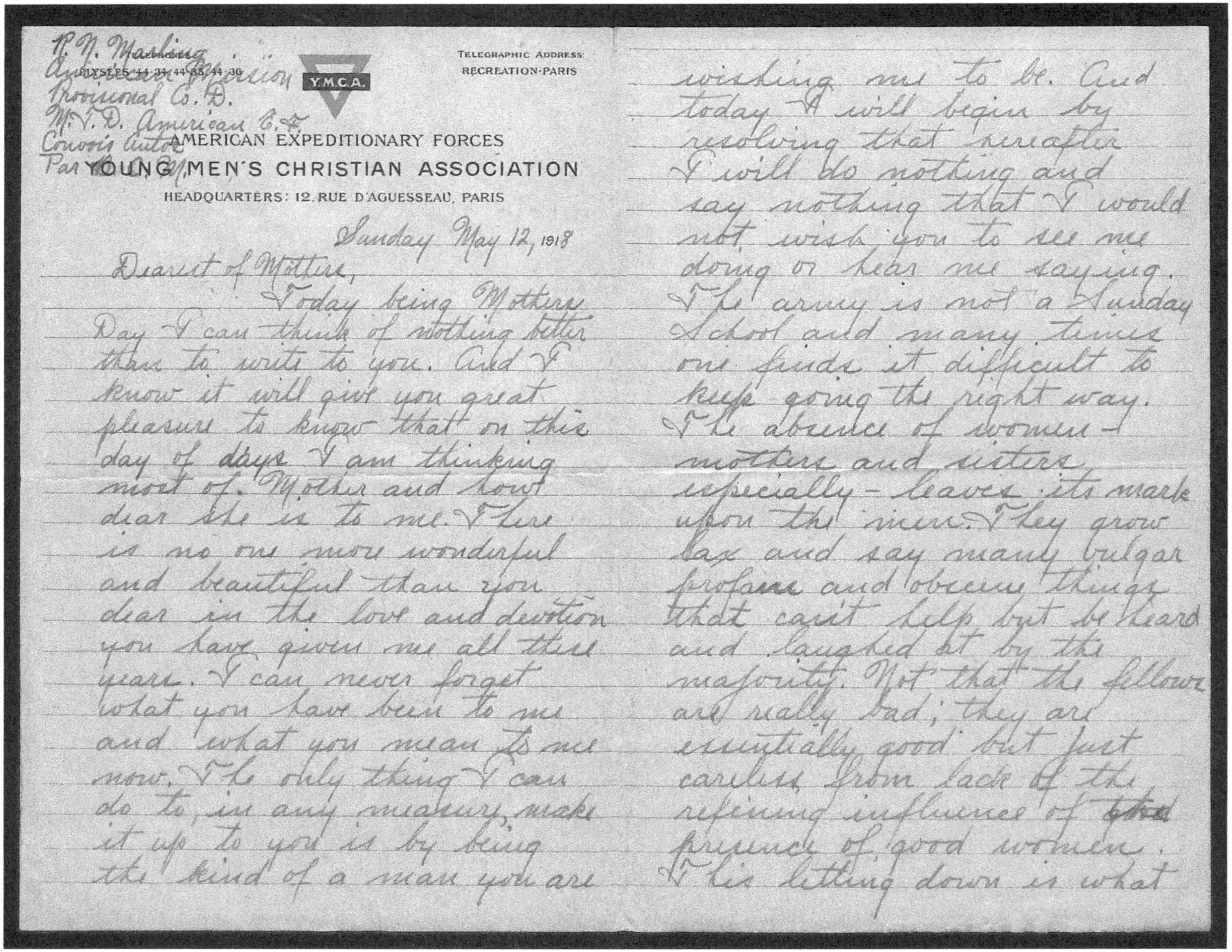

R. N. Marling
American Mission
Provisional Co. D.
M.T.D. American E.F.
Convois Autos
Par B.C.M.

TELEPHONES
ELYSEES 44-31 44-35 44-36

Y.M.C.A.

TELEGRAPHIC ADDRESS
RECREATION-PARIS

AMERICAN EXPEDITIONARY FORCES
YOUNG MEN'S CHRISTIAN ASSOCIATION
HEADQUARTERS: 12, RUE D'AGUESSEAU, PARIS

Sunday May 12, 1918

Dearest of Mothers,

Today being Mothers Day I can think of nothing better than to write to you. And I know it will give you great pleasure to know that on this day of days I am thinking most of Mother and how dear she is to me. There is no one more wonderful and beautiful than you dear in the love and devotion you have given me all these years. I can never forget what you have been to me and what you mean to me now. The only thing I can do to, in any measure, make it up to you is by being the kind of a man you are wishing me to be. And today I will begin by resolving that hereafter I will do nothing and say nothing that I would not wish you to see me doing or hear me saying. The army is not a Sunday School and many times one finds it difficult to keep going the right way. The absence of women — mothers and sisters especially — leaves its mark upon the men. They grow lax and say many vulgar profane and obscene things that can't help but be heard and laughed at by the majority. Not that the fellows are really bad; they are essentially good but just careless from lack of the refining influence of ~~the~~ presence of good women. This letting down is what

TELEPHONES: ÉLYSÉES 44-34, 44-35, 44-36

Y.M.C.A.

TELEGRAPHIC ADDRESS: RECREATION-PARIS

AMERICAN EXPEDITIONARY FORCES

YOUNG MEN'S CHRISTIAN ASSOCIATION

HEADQUARTERS: 12, RUE D'AGUESSEAU, PARIS

191

I will have to guard against.

Your lastest letter, that of April fourth, containing the letter from Howard Sherman was received several days ago. I was mighty glad to hear from you both. Howard has finally succeeded in getting into the army in the Ordnance Department and is going to an Army Ordnance School in Texas according to his letter. The same day I got your letter I also heard from Edith Smith, Elizabeth Head and Aunt Amy. Quite a choice collection for one day. Since then I have received but one letter and that day before yesterday, from father. He wrote a splendid long letter and enclosed a money order for ten "bucks" an Easter present. I must write to him today and thank him.

I've just been looking over the letters I have received and find that there are about eight people I will have to write to today if I am to catch up. They are to Elizabeth, Ruth Johnson, Aunt Ada, William, Howard Sherman, Jack Robson, Grandmother Marling and Farnham and a few others, not forgetting father. I may not be able to get them all off today but I'll try to get them written as soon as possible. Then I must not forget William next Sunday for it will be May seventeenth and he will be twenty-three years

AMERICAN
Y.M.C.A.
PASSED AS CENSORED
A.E.F.
A. 170

R. N. Marling
American Mission
Provisional Co. D.
M.T.D. American E.F.
Autos, Par B.C.M.

AMERICAN Y.M.C.A.

ON ACTIVE SERVICE
WITH THE
AMERICAN EXPEDITIONARY FORCE

May 19, 1918

Dear Mother,

Yesterday we had an inspection of trucks by Captain Langois, who is head of our groupement - French Army of course - and by Lieut Vincent in charge of of our groupe, together with several other French officers and our lieutenant. They were very much pleased with the showing we made, and consequently, today we have nothing to do but loaf and write. This morning I hiked over to the aviation field, and was very much interested in a new type of plane they have over there. It is a wonderful fighting plane with a speed of 235 kilometers per hour (about 147 miles per hour or almost 2½ miles per minute) and although it has been used little up to date, it is said to be greatly feared by the Huns. I'd like to see it in action - I mean in an air battle. I have seen it several times in the air, and it seems to have an edge on the Spad, although not as safe.

Your letters of April 18th and 26th were received day before yesterday, and were mighty welcome. The same day I received letters from father, William, and Marguerite. Father's contained a money order for $30, for

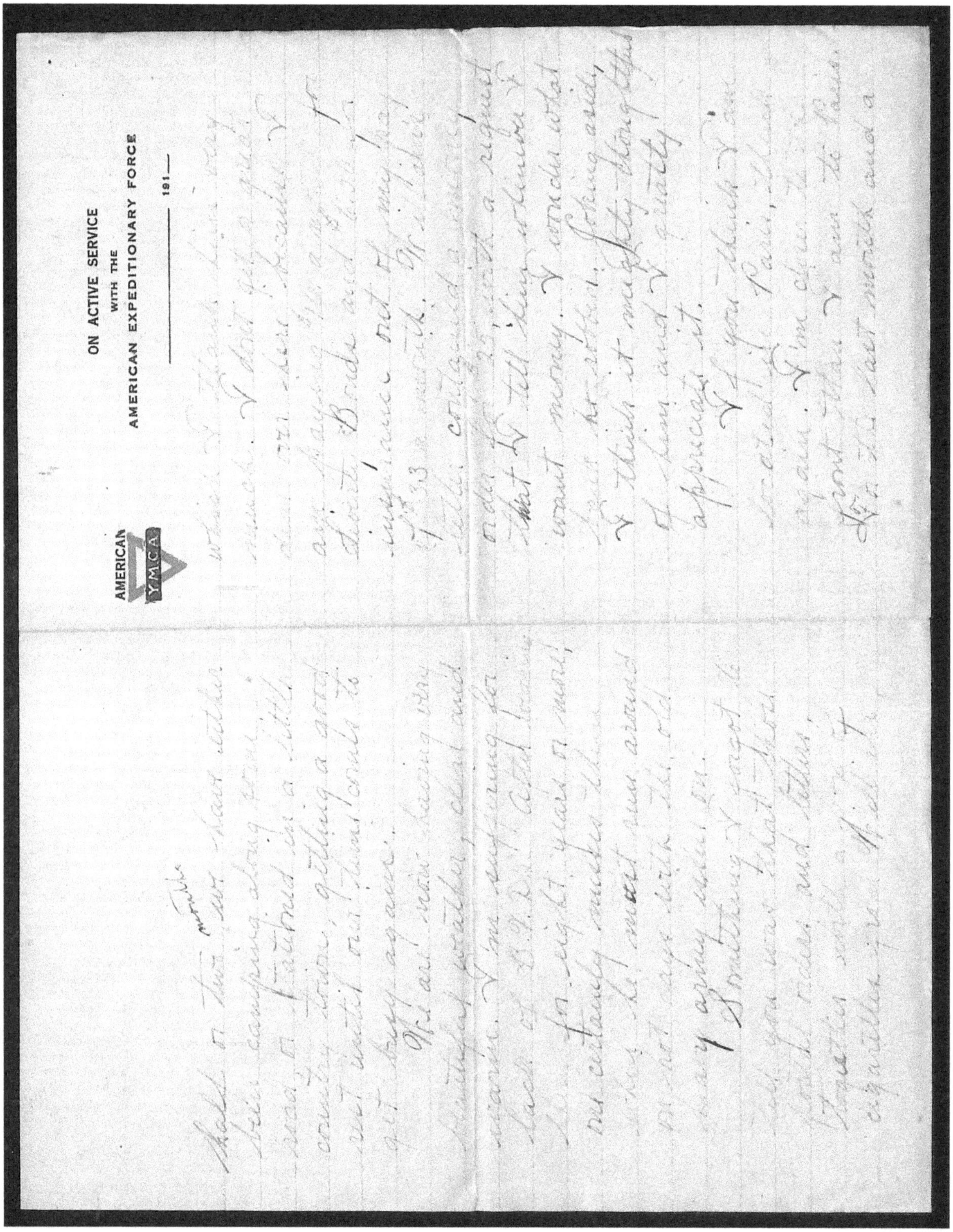

ON ACTIVE SERVICE
WITH THE
AMERICAN EXPEDITIONARY FORCE

______________ 191__

which I thank him very
much. I don't get a great
deal over here because I
am paying $16 a month for
Liberty Bonds and $6 for
insurance out of my pay
of $33 a month. Will's last
letter contained a money
order for $25, with a request
that I tell him whenever I
want money. I wonder what
[illegible] he robbed. Joking aside,
I think it mighty thoughtful
of him and I greatly
appreciate it.

If you think I'm
located in Paris, think
again. I'm closer to the
front than I am to Paris.
In the last month and a
half or two months we have either
been camping along some
road or stationed in a little
country town, getting a good
rest until our turns comes to
get busy again.

We are now having very
beautiful weather, clear and
warm. I'm suffering for
lack of B.V.D.'s. After wearing
them for eight years or more,
one certainly misses them
when he must run around
on hot days with the old
heavy army issue on.

Something I forgot to
tell you was that those
postal orders and letters,
together with a box of
cigarettes from Will [illegible]

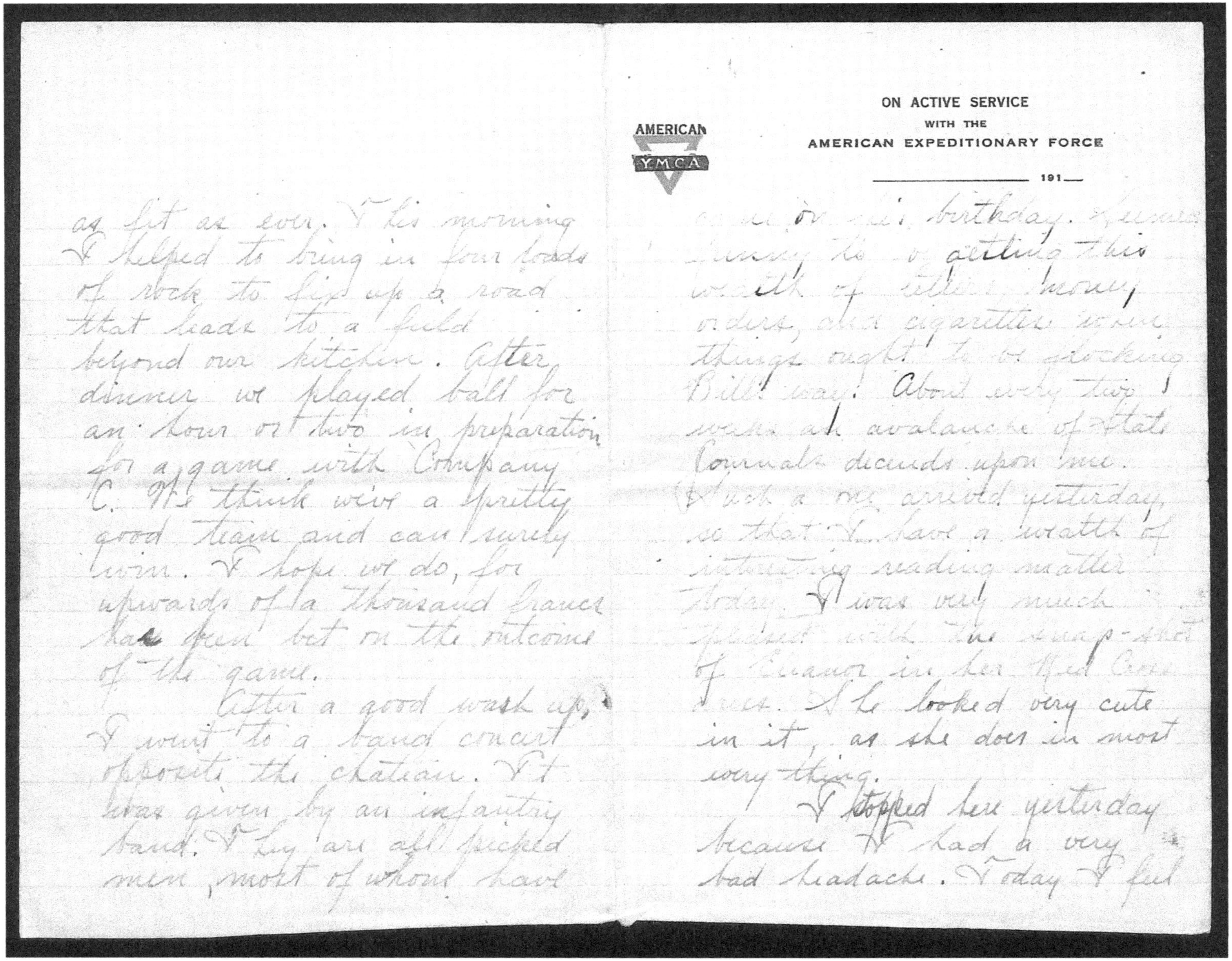

ON ACTIVE SERVICE
WITH THE
AMERICAN EXPEDITIONARY FORCE

__________ 191__

came on [illegible] birthday. It seems funny to be getting this wealth of letters, money orders, and cigarettes when things ought to be stocking Bill's way! About every two weeks an avalanche of State Journals descends upon me. Such a one arrived yesterday, so that I have a wealth of interesting reading matter today. I was very much pleased with the snap-shot of Eleanor in her Red Cross dress. She looked very cute in it, as she does in most every thing.

I stopped here yesterday because I had a very bad headache. Today I feel as fit as ever. This morning I helped to bring in four loads of rock to fix up a road that leads to a field beyond our kitchen. After dinner we played ball for an hour or two in preparation for a game with Company C. We think we've a pretty good team and can surely win. I hope we do, for upwards of a thousand francs has been bet on the outcome of the game.

After a good wash up, I went to a band concert opposite the chateau. It was given by an infantry band. They are all picked men, most of whom have

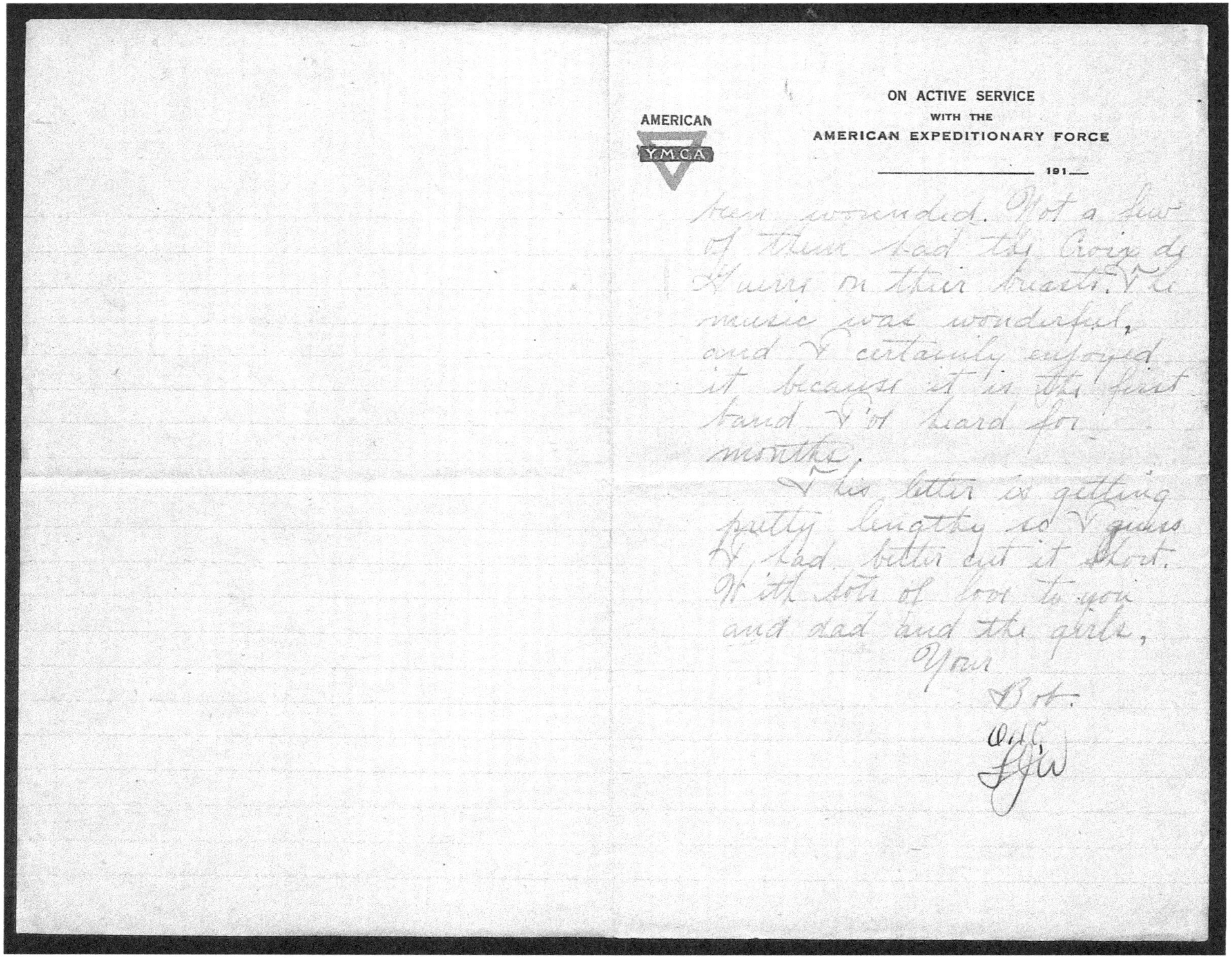
ON ACTIVE SERVICE
WITH THE
AMERICAN EXPEDITIONARY FORCE

AMERICAN Y.M.C.A.

______ 191__

been wounded. Not a few of them had the Croix de Guerre on their breasts. The music was wonderful, and I certainly enjoyed it because it is the first band I've heard for months.

This letter is getting pretty lengthy so I guess I had better cut it short. With lots of love to you and dad and the girls,

Your
Bob.

O.K.
LJW

YMCA

MAY 24, 1918

Last letter April 19

Info on Helen & George Engagement

friendship of 8 years

"K" looking for a man + wants KNM to bring one back

NOT IN PARIS

Many comments on letters received.

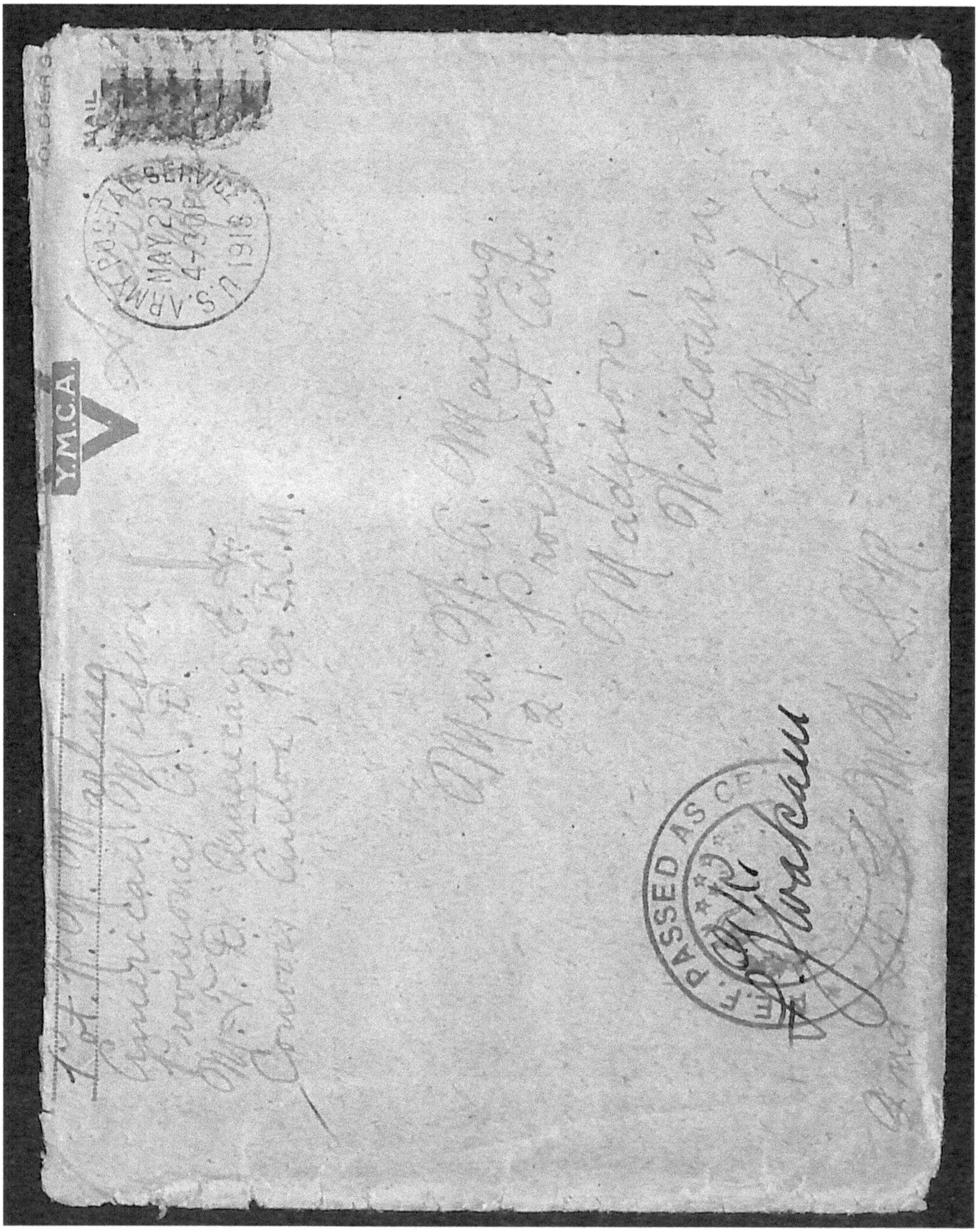
Y.M.C.A.
U.S. ARMY POSTAL SERVICE
MAY 23
4-30P
1918
MAIL
PASSED AS CE

R. M. Marling
American Mission
Provisional Co. B.
R. R. [illegible]
[illegible] Autos
Par B. C. M.

NATIONAL WAR WORK COUNCIL
YOUNG MEN'S CHRISTIAN ASSOCIATIONS
OF THE UNITED STATES
"WITH THE COLORS"

Friday, May 24th 1918.

Dear Mother,

I certainly took your last letter a long time to get here. It was dated April 19th and came yesterday. The day before I received a letter from Katherine dated April 24th with the startling announcement of Helen's & George's engagement. I was nearly taken off my feet - so unexpected - after their short "friendship" of about eight years. Today I received a letter from Helen herself, written May first, and it is a scream. Nothing but George's & "I's" and rings - sleepless nights and exclamations, with a generous sprinkling of "Bob dear's". I've been laughing over it all day long.

NATIONAL WAR WORK COUNCIL

YOUNG MEN'S CHRISTIAN ASSOCIATIONS

OF THE UNITED STATES

"WITH THE COLORS"

Helen said in her letter "K" is still looking for a man — and I'm afraid she'll look a long time for none are good enough for her." K seems very much worried over it too. She wants me to find a nice man for her over here and bring him home with me. With this request she sends a very good recommendation of her domestic qualities.

If you will notice Paris, France is no longer attached to my address. It has been dropped for some time. Paris was merely a distributing point for mail, I was never located there — as I have told you and father in letters that are now on the way.

I received a letter from

NATIONAL WAR WORK COUNCIL

YOUNG MEN'S CHRISTIAN ASSOCIATIONS

OF THE UNITED STATES

"WITH THE COLORS"

Ruth today dated May 3rd - only twenty one days on the way not bad at all coming all the way from Wisconsin. Ruth is quite filled with the spirit of service, tried to take the training for nurses and come over here but found she was to young and that they would not make any exceptions. So she is going to continue at the U. until she is old enough to enter the course of training.

Every one that write to me tells me of the seriousness of Dud Davis' injuries. Helen says that he is now on the way home. Is it really true? Or is he still over here in the hospital?

Goodbye dear mother Love, Bob.

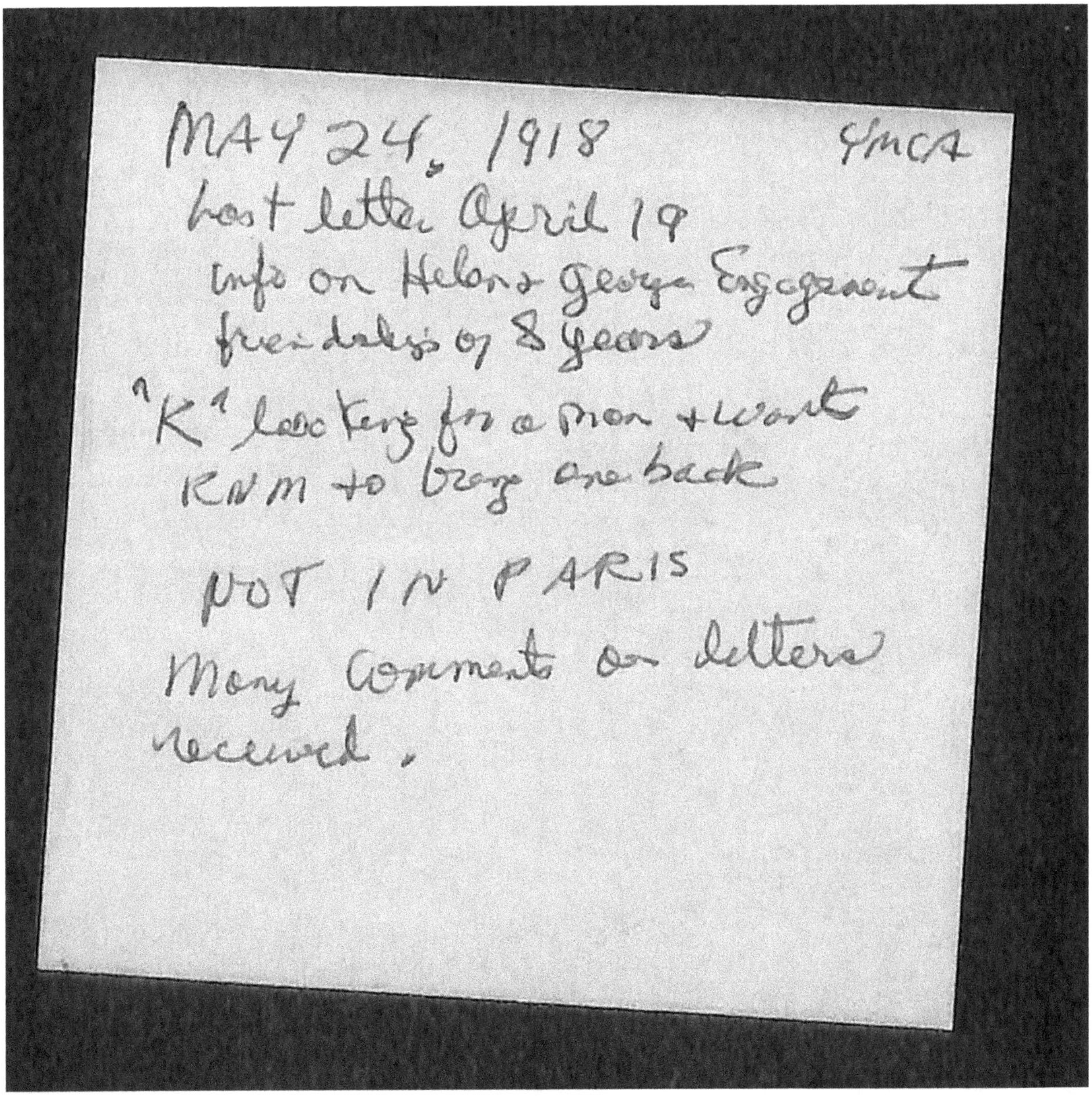

MAY 24, 1918 YMCA

Last letter April 19

Info on Helen & George Engagement

friendship of 8 years

"K" looking for a man + wants

KNM to bring one back

NOT IN PARIS

Many comments on letters

received.

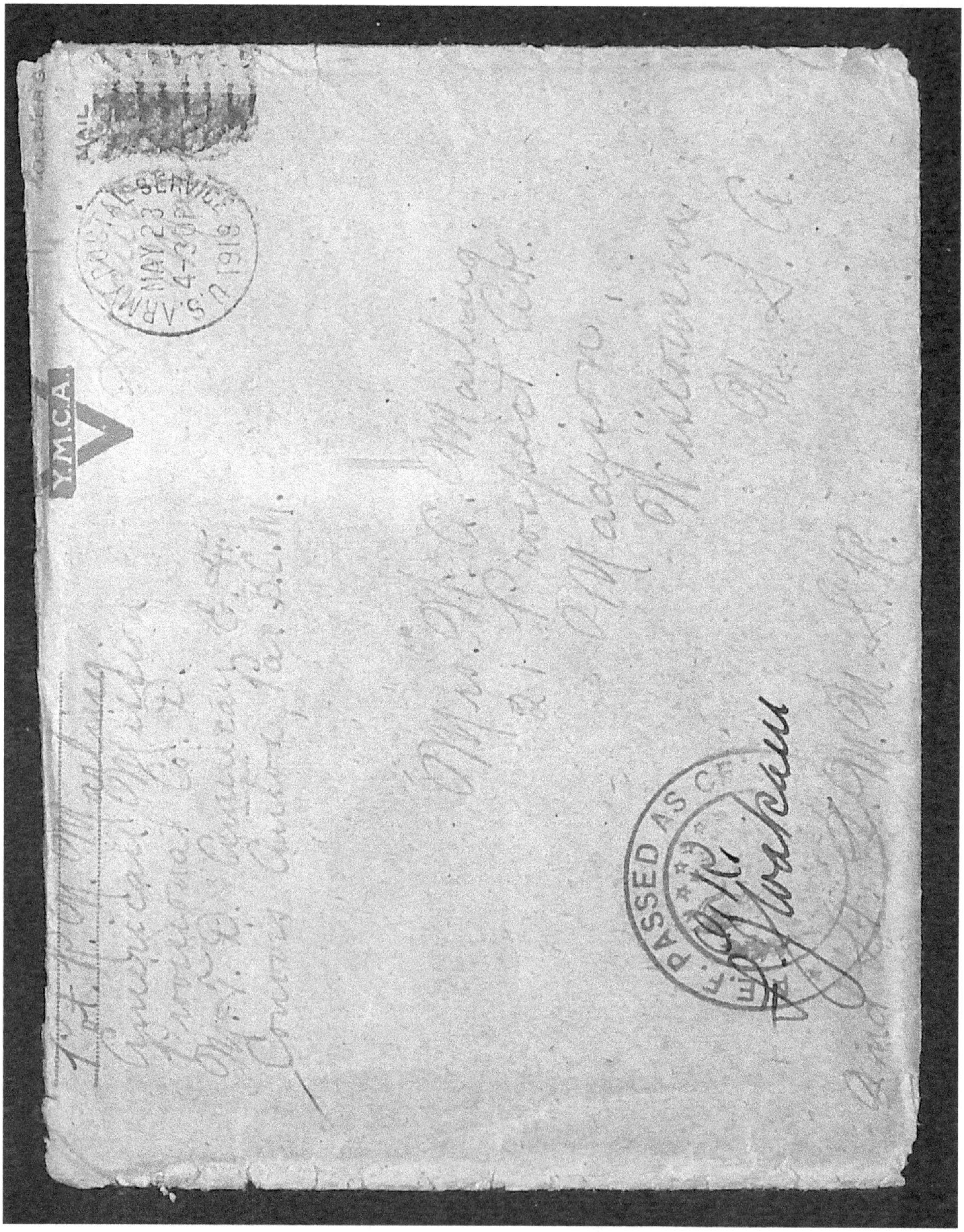
U.S. ARMY POSTAL SERVICE
MAY 23
4-30P
1919
Y.M.C.A.
PASSED AS C

R. N. Marling
American Mission
Provisional Co. D.
[illegible]
[illegible]
Par. B. C. M.

NATIONAL WAR WORK COUNCIL
YOUNG MEN'S CHRISTIAN ASSOCIATIONS
OF THE UNITED STATES
"WITH THE COLORS"

Friday, May 24th 1918.

Dear Mother,

I certainly took your last letter a long time to get here. It was dated April 19th and came yesterday. The day before I received a letter from Katherine dated April 24th with the startling announcement of Helen's & George's engagement. I was nearly taken off my feet - so unexpected - after their short "friendship" of about eight years. Today I received a letter from Helen herself, written May first, and it is a scream. Nothing but George's & "I's" and rings - sleepless nights and exclamations, with a generous sprinkling of "Bob dear"'s. I've been laughing over it all day long.

NATIONAL WAR WORK COUNCIL

YOUNG MEN'S CHRISTIAN ASSOCIATIONS

OF THE UNITED STATES

"WITH THE COLORS"

Helen said in her letter "K" is still looking for a man — and I'm afraid she'll look a long time for none are good enough for her." "K" seems very much worried over it too. She wants me to find a nice man for her over here and bring him home with me. With this request she sends a very good recommendation of her domestic qualities.

If you will notice Paris, France is no longer attached to my address. It has been dropped for some time. Paris was merely a distributing point for mail, I was never located there — as I have told you and father in letters that are now on the way.

I received a letter from

NATIONAL WAR WORK COUNCIL

YOUNG MEN'S CHRISTIAN ASSOCIATIONS

OF THE UNITED STATES

"WITH THE COLORS"

Ruth today dated May 3d - only twenty-one days on the way not bad at all coming all the way from Wisconsin. Ruth is quite filled with the spirit of service, tried to take the training for nurses and come over here, but found she was to young and that they would not make any exceptions. So she is going to continue at the U. until she is old enough to enter the course of training.

Every one that write to me tells me of the seriousness of Dud Davis' injuries. Helen says that he is now on the way home. Is it really true? Or is he still over here in the hospital?

Goodbye dear mother Love, Bob.

JUNE 5 & 11, 1918
2 POST CARDS
Truck is in for Repairs
& for new parts.
Hurt left Hand.

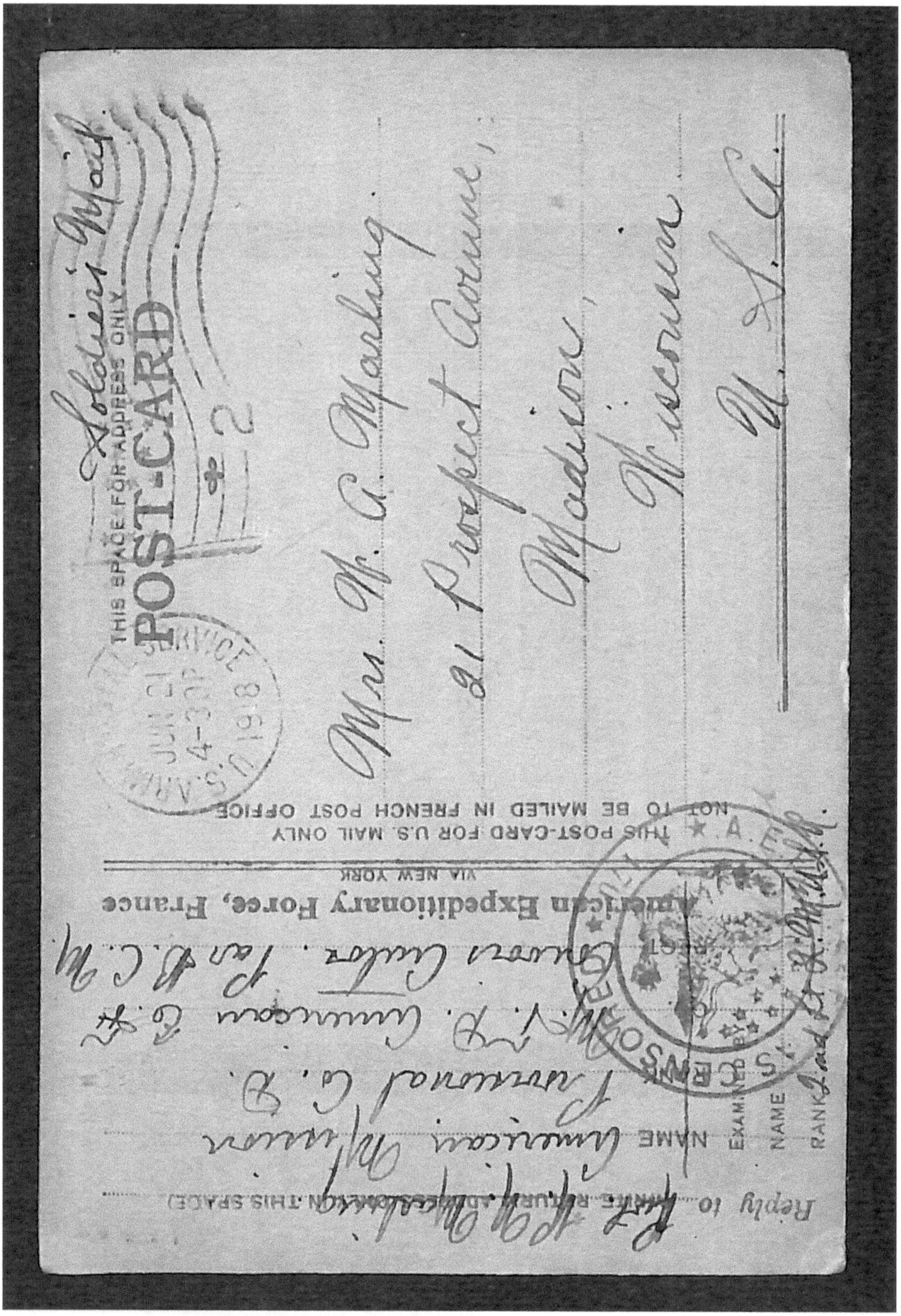
Soldier's Mail
THIS SPACE FOR ADDRESS ONLY
POST-CARD
U.S. ARMY ... SERVICE
JUN 21 4-30 P 1918
21 Prospect Avenue,
Madison,
Wisconsin
U. S. A.
American Expeditionary Force, France
VIA NEW YORK
THIS POST-CARD FOR U.S. MAIL ONLY
NOT TO BE MAILED IN FRENCH POST OFFICE
Reply to (WRITE RETURN ADDRESS ON THIS SPACE)
NAME
EXAMINED BY
NAME
RANK
CENSORED

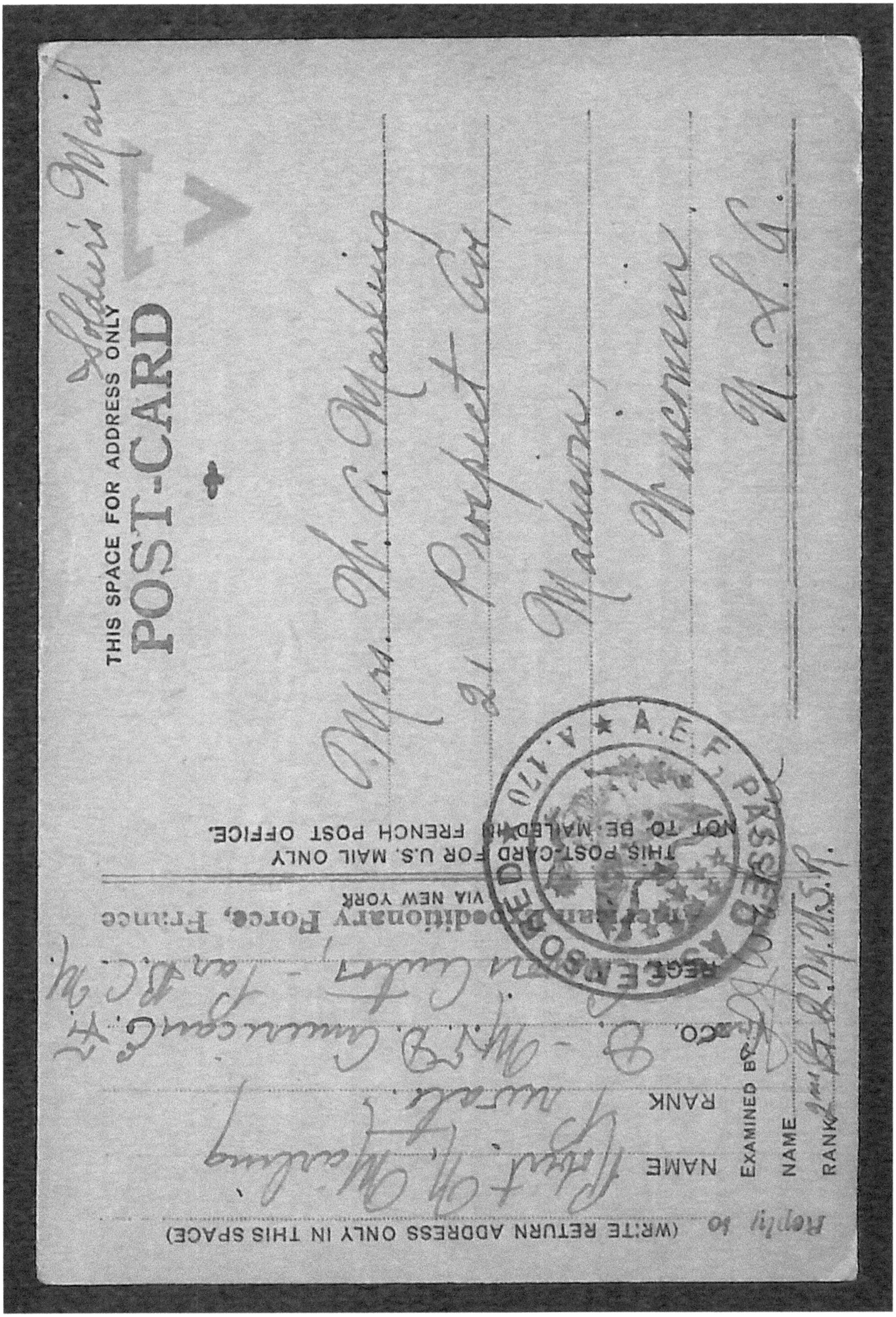
THIS SPACE FOR ADDRESS ONLY
POST-CARD
THIS POST-CARD FOR U.S. MAIL ONLY
NOT TO BE MAILED IN FRENCH POST OFFICE.
VIA NEW YORK
American Expeditionary Force, France
(WRITE RETURN ADDRESS ONLY IN THIS SPACE)
Reply to
NAME
RANK
CO.
REGT.
EXAMINED BY
NAME
RANK
A.E.F. PASSED AS CENSORED
A 170

June 23, 1918

Knights of Columbus.

WAR ACTIVITIES

Letter

Been sick of a week

high fever & influenza

5 days in infirmary

"Salts & Castor oil"

Italians are doing well

against Austrians.

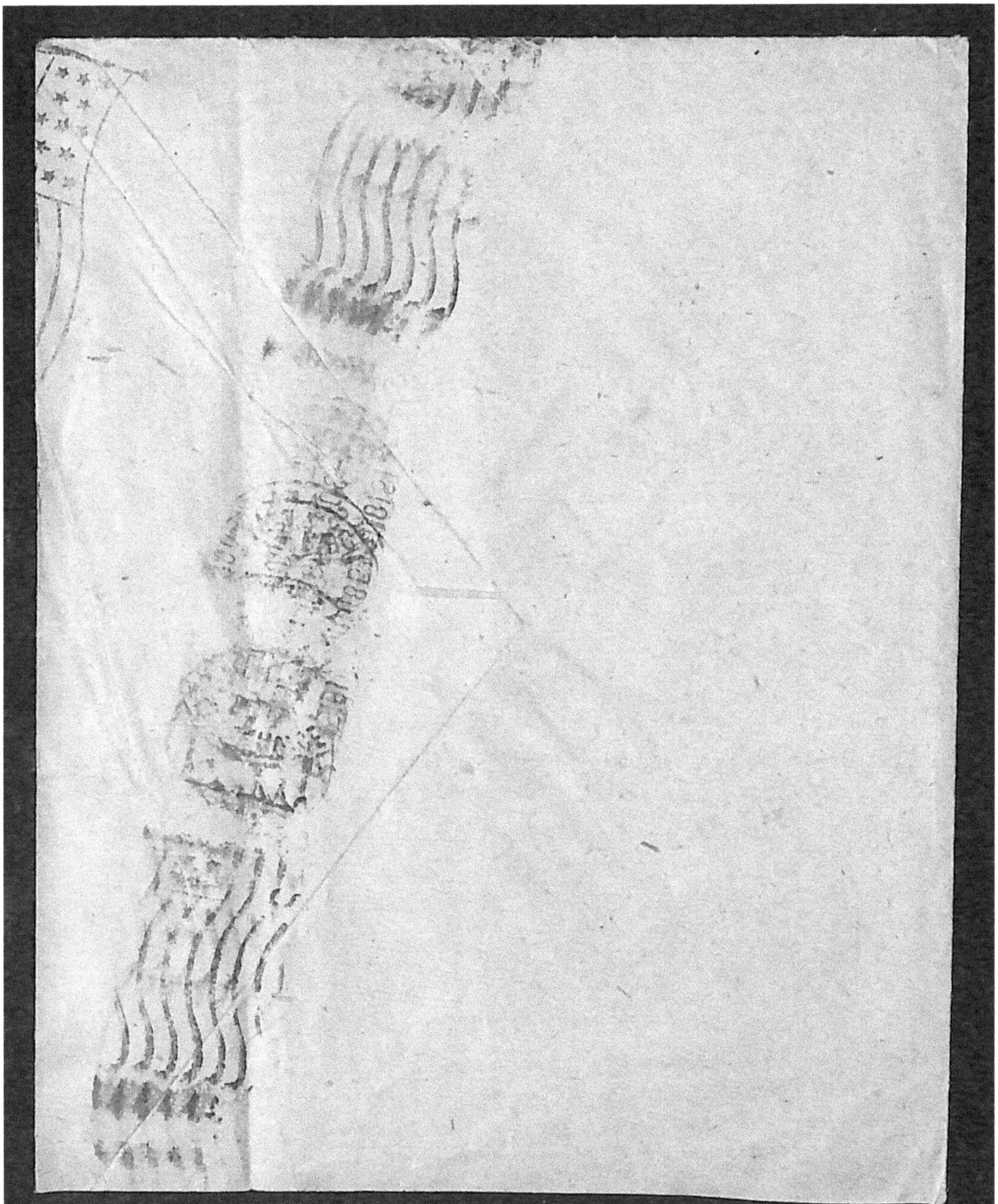

Pvt. R. N. Marble
American Mission
Provisional Co D.
M. T. D. - A. E. F.
Convois Autos
[illegible] B. C. M.

KNIGHTS OF COLUMBUS

WAR ACTIVITIES

K of C

CAMP ....

June 23d 1918

Dear Mother,

You may wonder why this paper. I couldn't find any Y. M. C. A. paper handy and as there seemed to be an over supply of this I made use of it. I've been sick for about a week with something like influenza and a good dose of it with pretty high fever. Just released from the infirmary today after five days in bed. I am feeling fine now although a little weak from fever - and salts and castor oil.

The Italians are doing finely against the Austrians, and every one seems to think the war will end in a year. At least they are talking that way. Now let us begin to drive back the Germans and I will be ready to believe that I'll be home a year from now. Every-one seems to speak highly of the fighting quality of our boys. The Germans themselves are beginning to think much the same according ~~from~~ to dope picked up from prisoners now and then. Am well and happy and send to all of you my love,

Your affectionate son,
Bob.
AMC

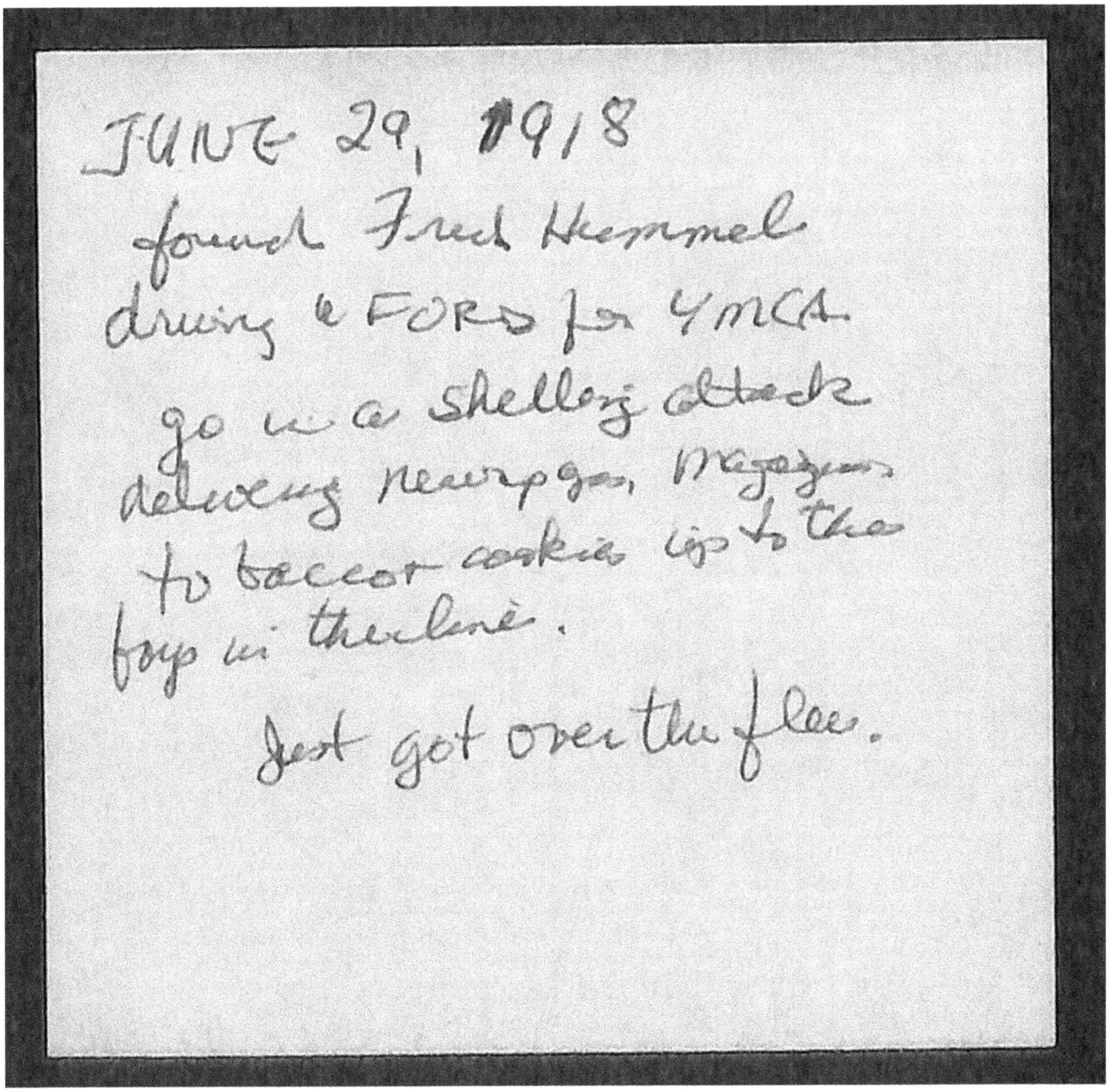
JUNE 29, 1918
found Fred Hemmel
driving a FORD for YMCA
go in a shelling attack
delivering newspapers, magazines
tobacco cookies up to the
boys in the line.
Just got over the flu.

AMERICAN
Y.M.C.A.
SOLDIER'S
MAIL
PASSED AS CENSORED

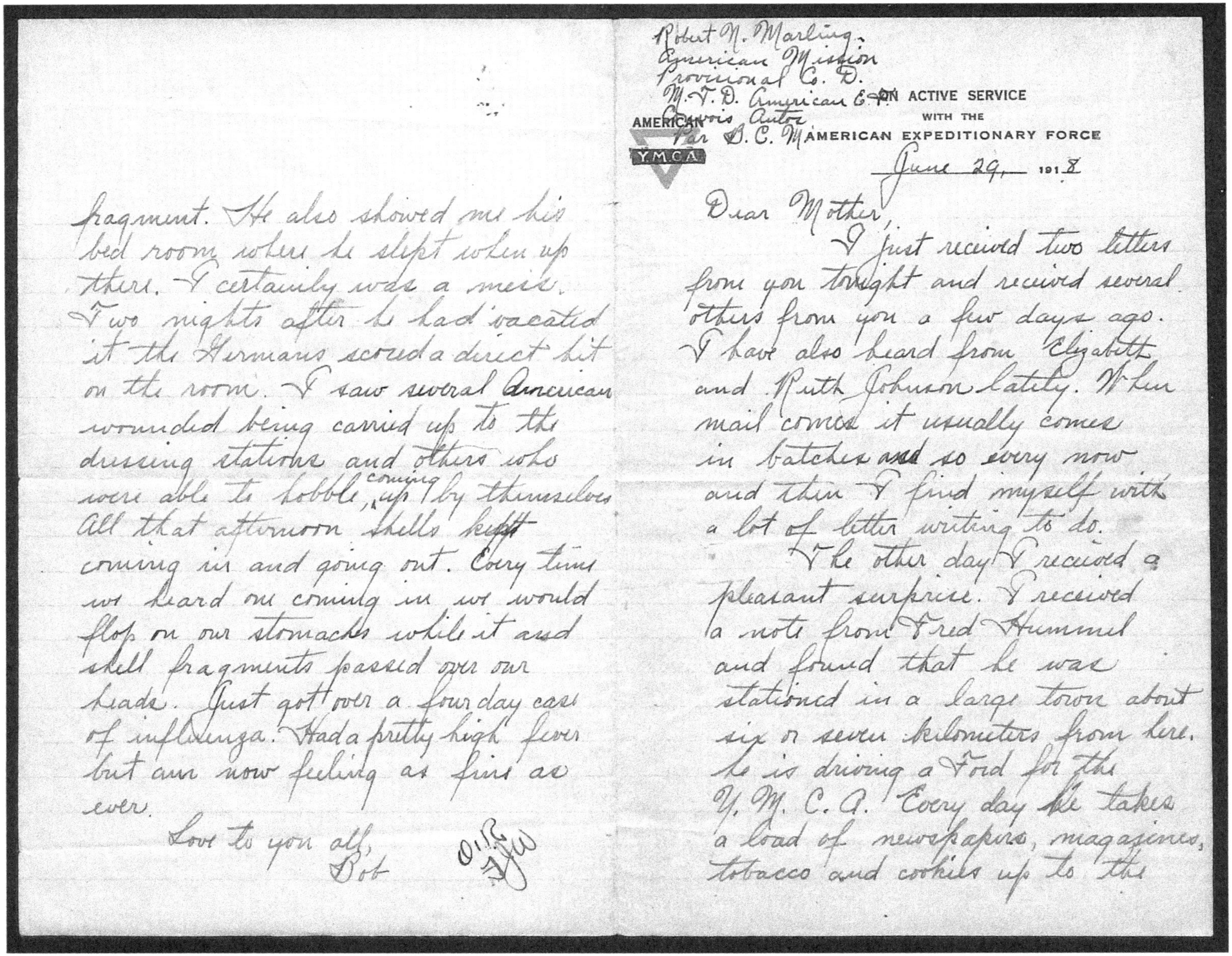

Robert N. Marling.
American Mission
Provisional C. D.
M. T. D. American E. F.
Convois Autos
Par B. C. M.

AMERICAN Y.M.C.A. ON ACTIVE SERVICE WITH THE AMERICAN EXPEDITIONARY FORCE

June 29, 1918

Dear Mother,

I just received two letters from you tonight and received several others from you a few days ago. I have also heard from Elizabeth and Ruth Johnson lately. When mail comes it usually comes in batches ~~and~~ so every now and then I find myself with a lot of letter writing to do.

The other day I received a pleasant surprise. I received a note from Fred Hummel and found that he was stationed in a large town about six or seven kilometers from here. He is driving a Ford for the Y. M. C. A. Every day he takes a load of newspapers, magazines, tobacco and cookies up to the

fragment. He also showed me his bed room where he slept when up there. It certainly was a mess. Two nights after he had vacated it the Germans scored a direct hit on the room. I saw several American wounded being carried up to the dressing stations and others who were able to hobble, coming up by themselves. All that afternoon shells ~~kept~~ coming in and going out. Every time we heard one coming in we would flop on our stomachs while it and shell fragments passed over our heads. Just got over a four day case of influenza. Had a pretty high fever but am now feeling as fine as ever.

Love to you all,
Bob

O.K.
FJW

boys in the lines. He asked me in the note to come in and see him and take the trip up to the line with him. The other day I received permission to go in to town and I hunted up the Y.M.C.A. warehouse and found Fred just getting ready to start out. I was mighty glad to see him for he is the first real friend and "frat" brother that I have met over here. We had quite a talk about what every one was doing among the brothers and others, while we were putting in the stock of things to take up to the boys. We got started at about ten oclock and made the run up there in about an hour or an hour and a half. I was surprised to find so many Y.M.C.A's and secretaries right up in the thick of things. And they are in the thick of it for at present there is an average of about one secretary or "Y" man wounded or "knocked off" a day. Fred is always having close calls and is now quite expert at dodging shells - so he tells me. The other day he was driving along a road when a shell came up from behind him, took the top off of a hay stack he was nearly abreast of and exploded in the road about fifty yards ahead of him. Right up at the front where one has to abandon even a Ford, he took me over a road that the day before had been shelled at intervals of three minutes he showed me a spot where he had fallen down when he heard a shell coming and I'll swear ~~it~~ the shell hole wasn't more than twenty or twenty five feet away. Fred said that he put up his head after he heard it explode just to see how close it came, and together with a lot of dirt he got hit on the "~~tin~~ hat" by a shell

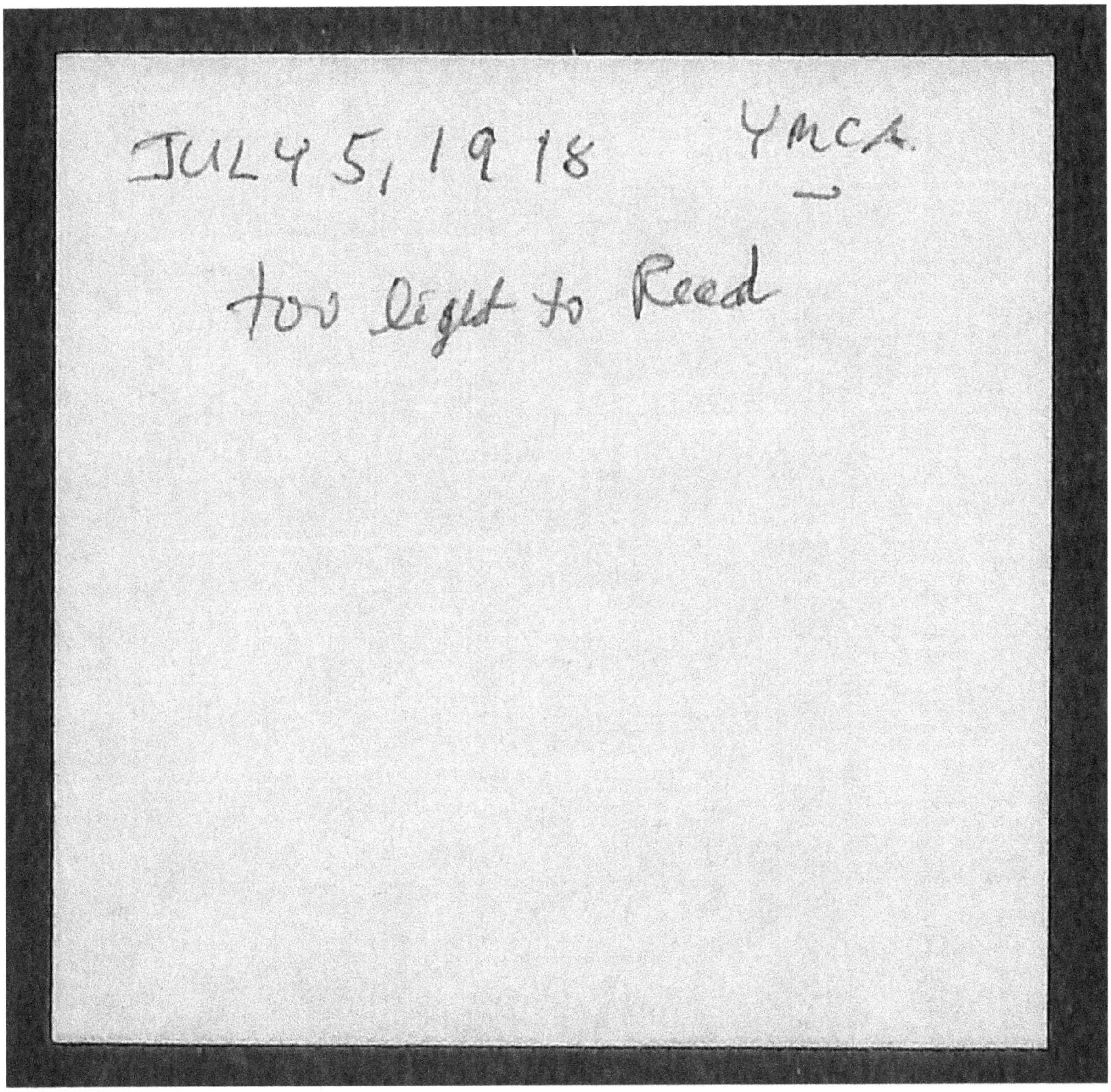

JULY 5, 1918 YMCA

too light to Read

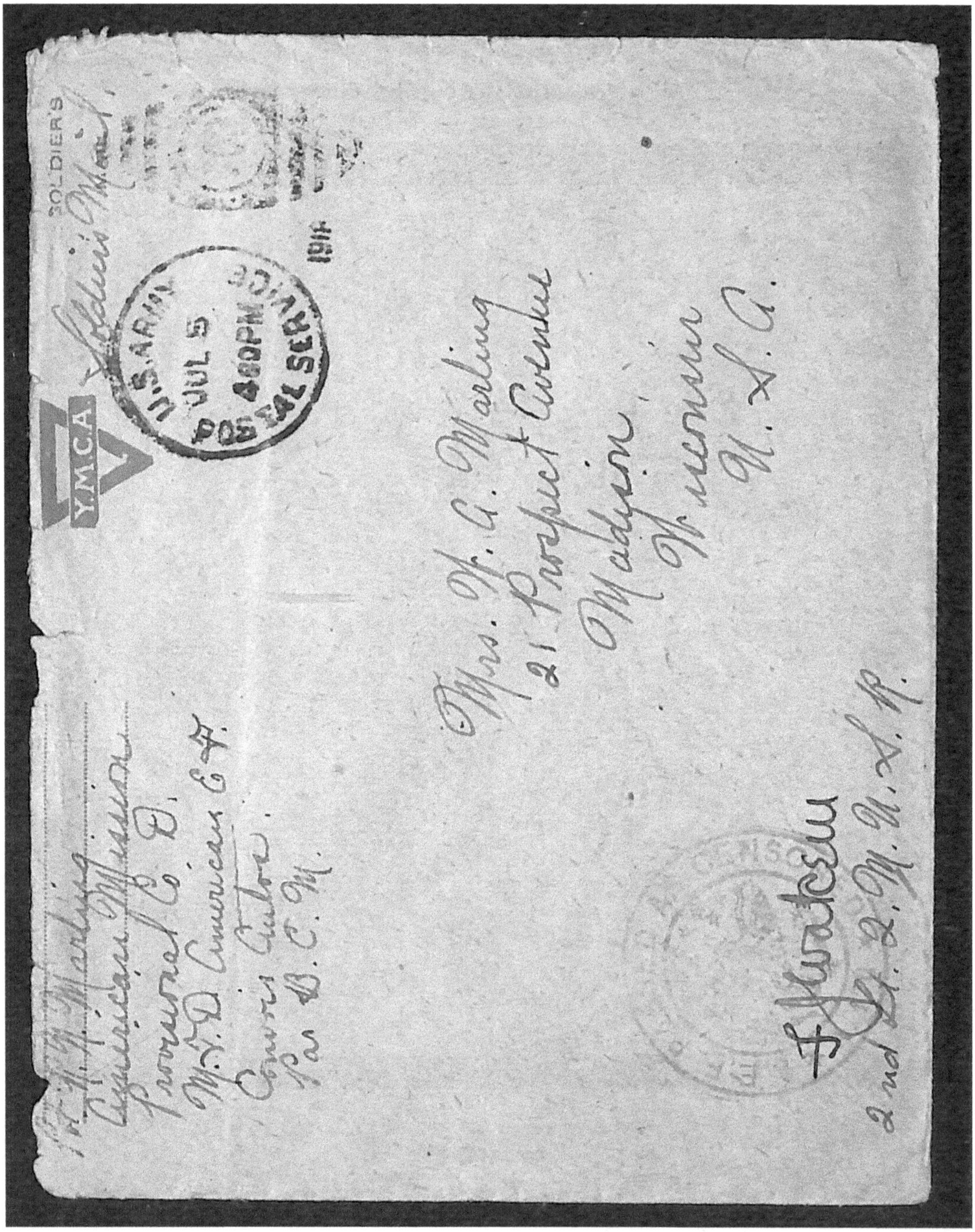
Y.M.C.A.
SOLDIER'S
U.S. ARMY POSTAL SERVICE
JUL 5
1918
Soldier's Mail
Mrs. F. A. Marling
21 Prospect Avenue
Madison
Wisconsin
U.S.A.

AMERICAN
YMCA
ON ACTIVE SERVICE
WITH THE
AMERICAN EXPEDITIONARY FORCE

some time to some for I seem

JULY 17, 1918

Le Foyer Du Soldat

UNION FRANCO-AMERICANE

Received Jan 23 letter

Sadie & Cecilia

Very breezy "rolling"

day & night – haystack

Very faint writing hard to

read.

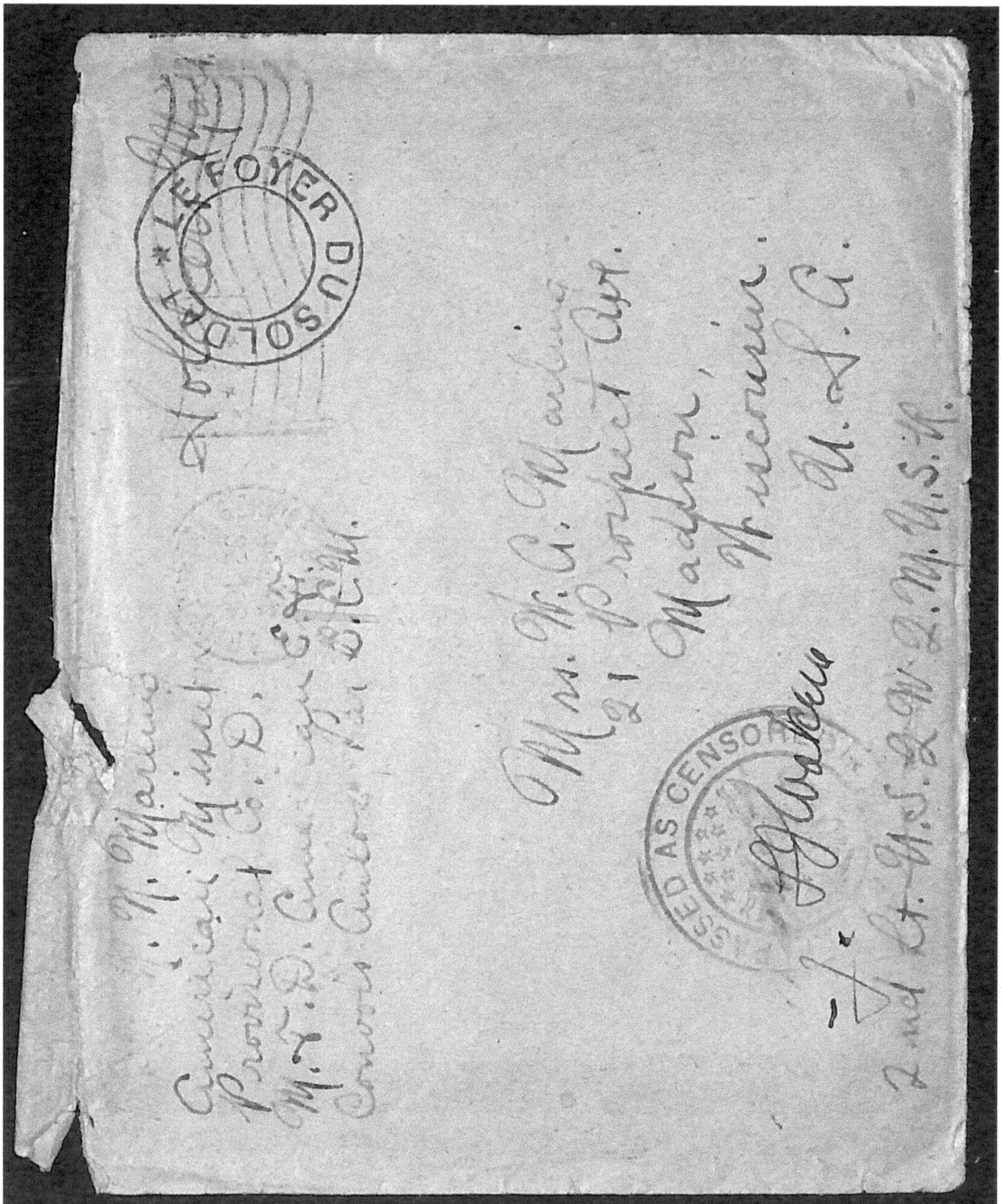
LE FOYER DU SOLDAT
ED AS CENSOR
21 Prospect Ave.
Madison,
Wisconsin,
U.S.A.

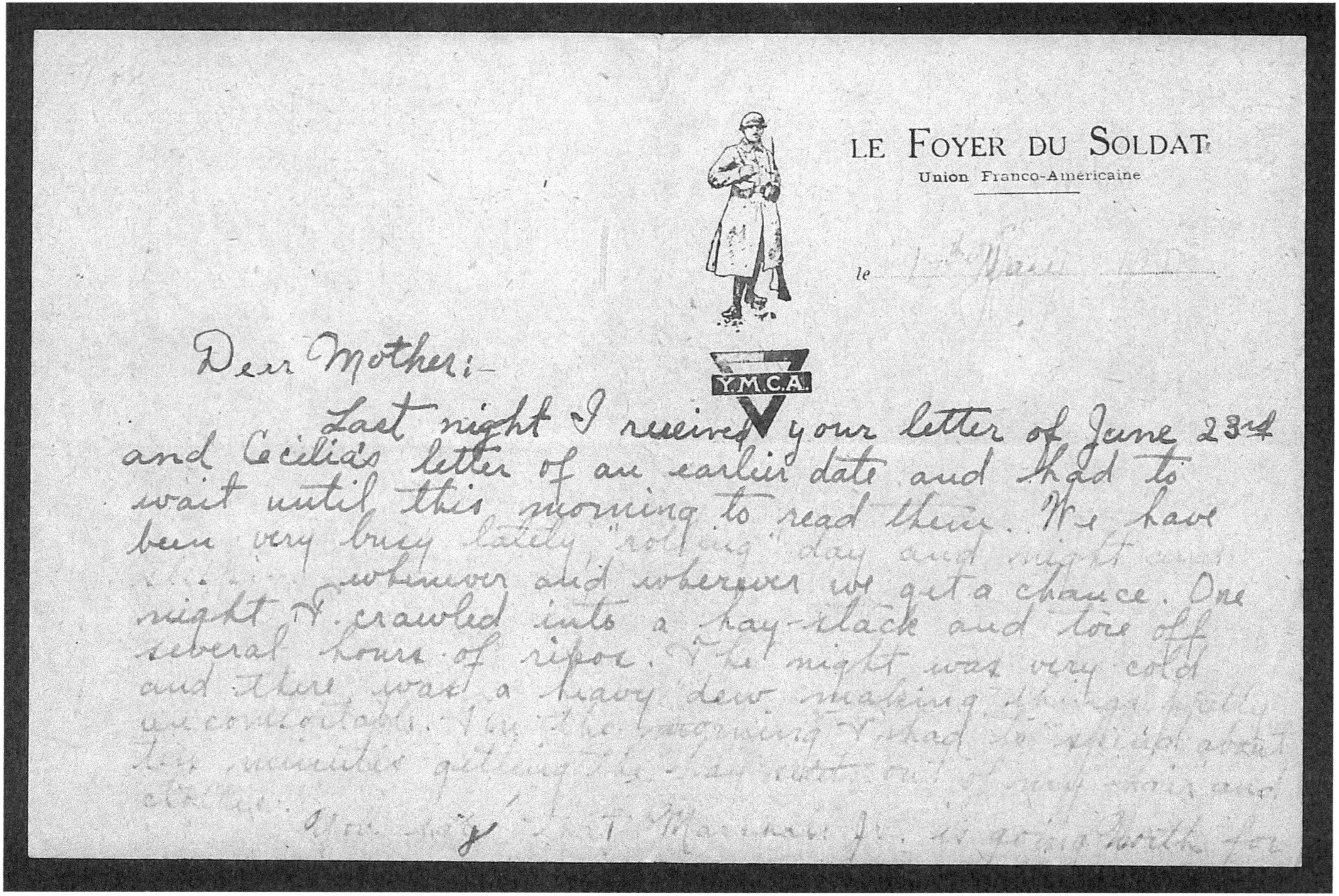
LE FOYER DU SOLDAT
Union Franco-Americaine

le [illegible]

Dear Mother:-

Last night I received your letter of June 23rd and Cecilia's letter of an earlier date and had to wait until this morning to read them. We have been very busy lately "rolling" day and night and [illegible] whenever and wherever we get a chance. One night I crawled into a hay-stack and tore off several hours of repose. The night was very cold and there was a heavy dew making things pretty uncomfortable. In the morning I had to spend about ten minutes getting the hay seeds out of my ears and clothes.

You say [illegible] Marsman Jr. is going with for

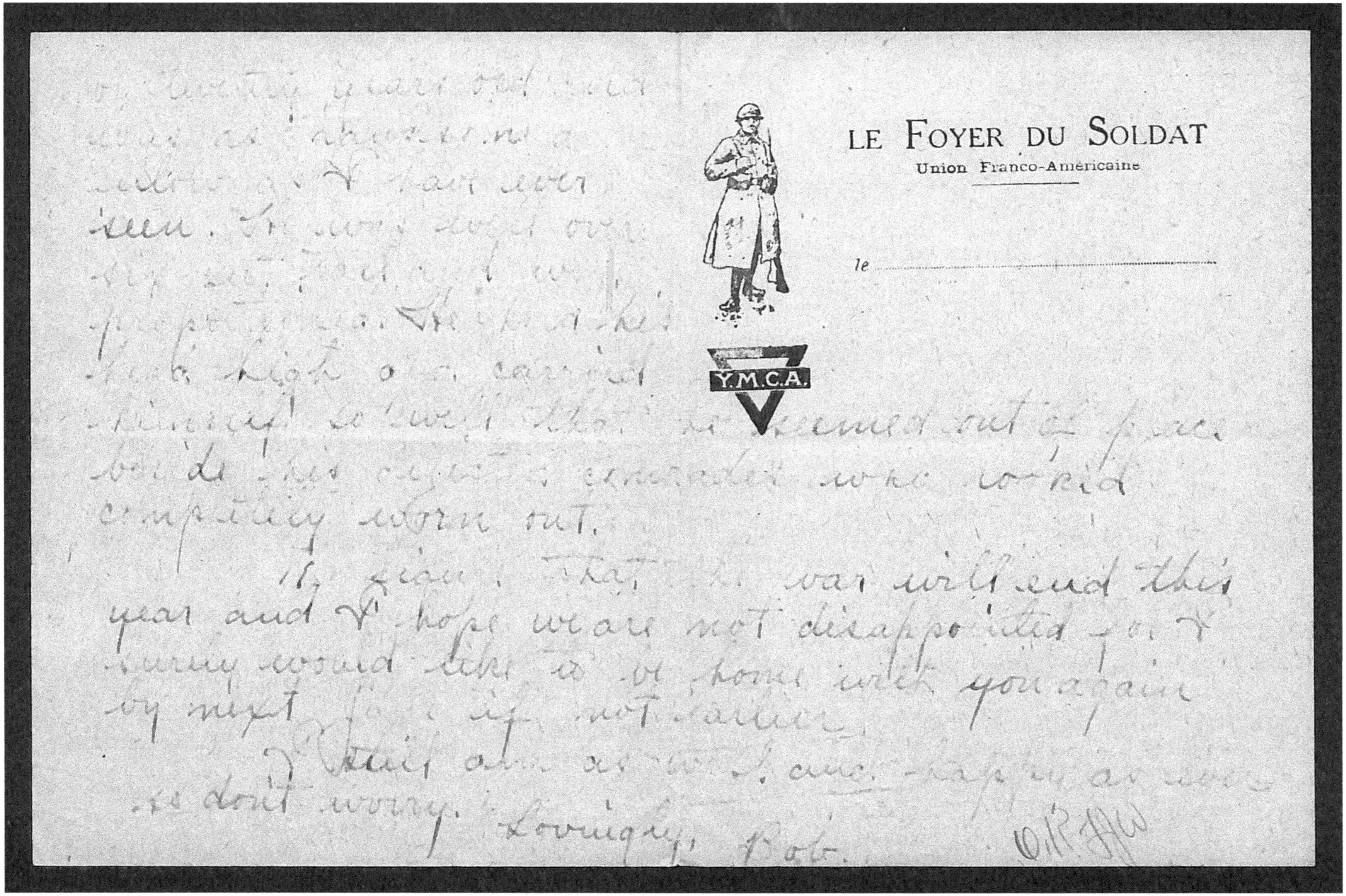

LE FOYER DU SOLDAT

Union Franco-Américaine

le ....

Y.M.C.A.

[illegible] twenty years old [illegible]
[illegible]
[illegible] I have ever
seen. [illegible] over
[illegible]
[illegible]
held high [illegible] carried
himself so well that he seemed out of place
beside his [illegible] comrades who looked
completely worn out.

[illegible] that the war will end this
year and I hope we are not disappointed for I
surely would like to be home with you again
by next [illegible] if not earlier.

[illegible] am as [illegible] I am happy as ever
so don't worry.

Lovingly, Bob.

O.R.H.W.

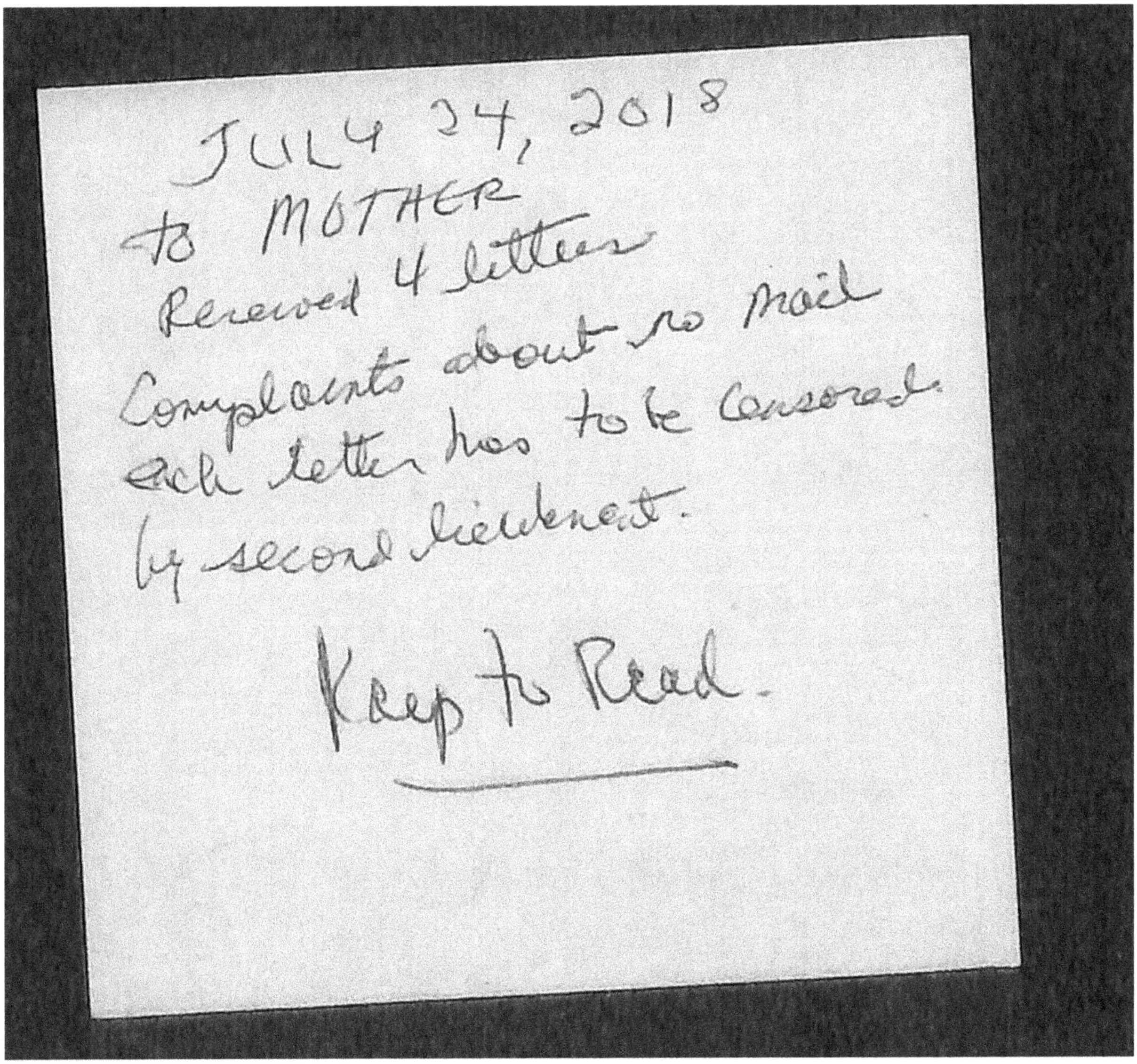
JULY 24, 2018
To MOTHER
Received 4 letters
Complaints about no mail
each letter has to be censored.
by second lieutenant.

Keep to Read.

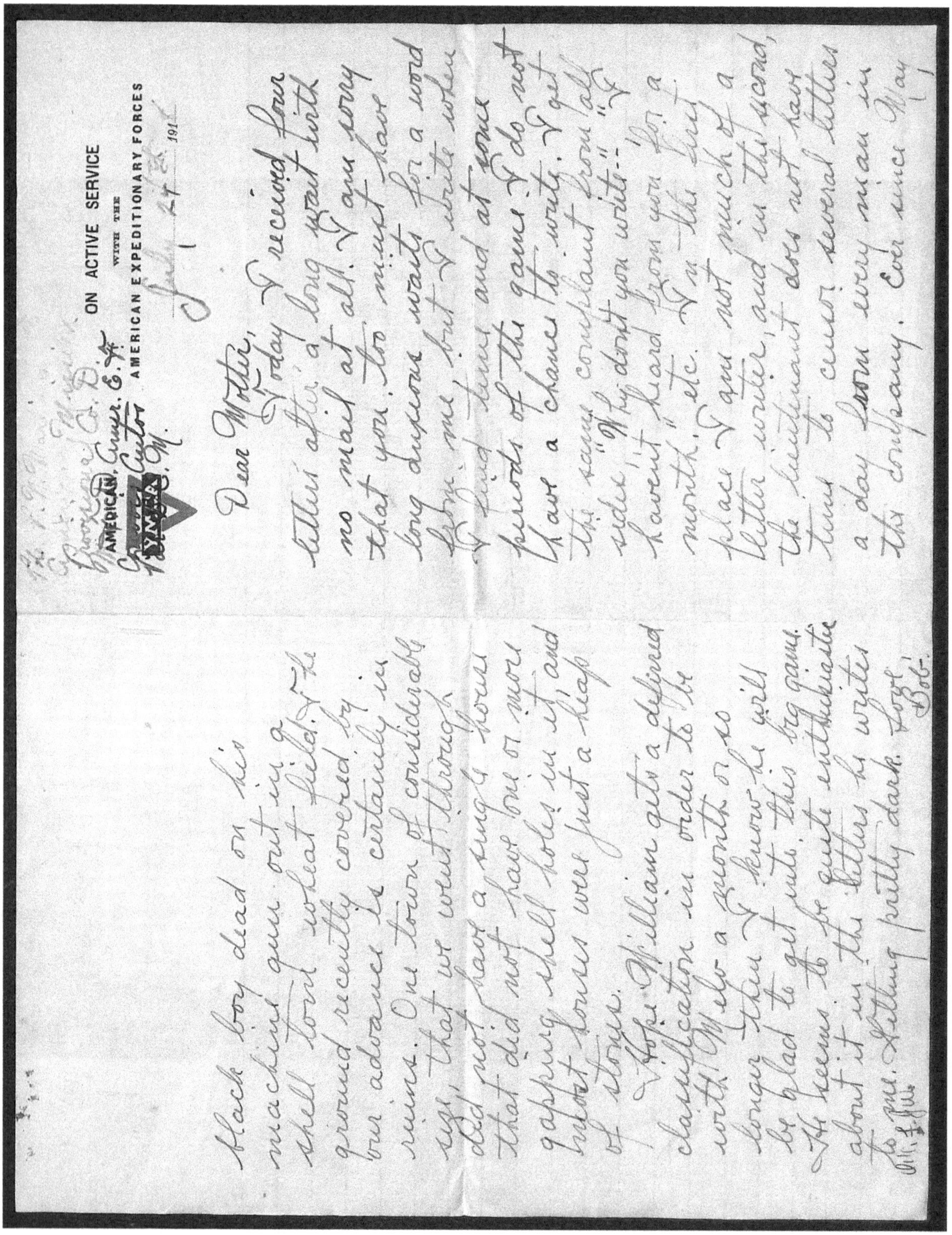

ON ACTIVE SERVICE
WITH THE
AMERICAN EXPEDITIONARY FORCES
AMERICAN Y.M.C.A.

Provisional Co. D.
Amer. E.F.

July 24th 1918

Dear Mother,
Today I received four letters after a long wait with no mail at all. I am sorry that you, too must have long anxious waits for a word from me, but I write when I find time and at some periods of the game I do not have a chance to write. I get the same complaint from all sides, "Why dont you write--", "I haven't heard from you for a month," etc. In the first place I am not much of a letter writer, and in the second, the lieutenant does not have time to censor several letters a day from every man in the company. Ever since May

black boy dead on his machine gun out in a shell torn wheat field. The ground recently covered by our advance is certainly in ruins. One town of considerable size, that we went through did not have a single house that did not have one or more gapping shell holes in it, and most houses were just a heap of stones.

Hope William gets a deferred classification in order to be with Melo a month or so longer then I know he will be glad to get into this big game. He seems to be quite enthusiastic about it in the letters he writes to me. Getting pretty dark. Love
Bob.

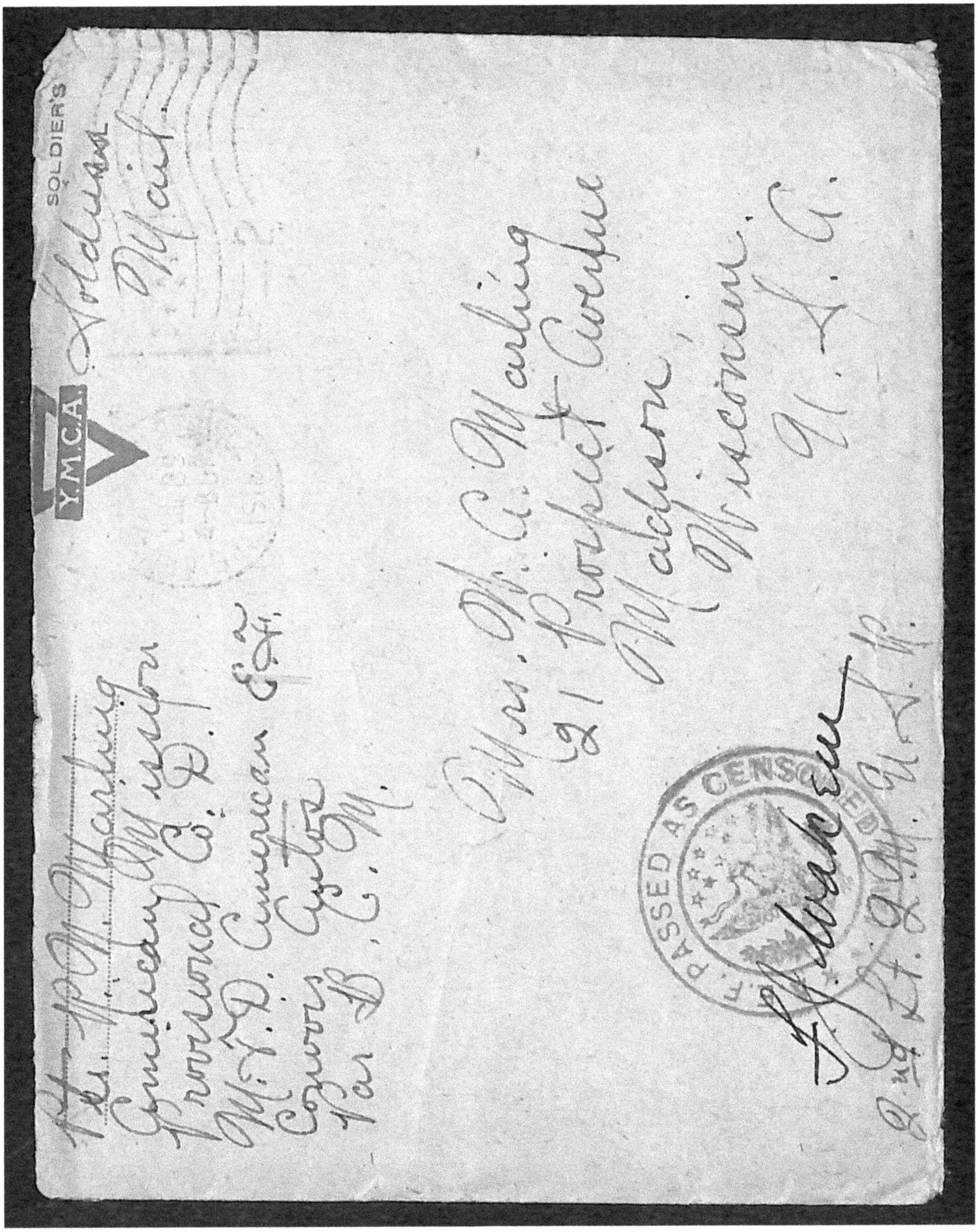
SOLDIER'S
Y.M.C.A.
PASSED AS CENSORED

on the list of Crew we have been worked pretty constantly, rolling at least every other day - on an average - and at times of great pressure it means work day and night. We must eat and sleep then when we have time and let correspondence wait. Even if each man did find time to write as often as those back home wish, remember the lieutenant needs rest also, for he must be out on every convoy and is out longer and more often than any one man on the trucks.

I've used a lot of words and paper in trying to say this; dont worry if you do not get letters when you expect them, as much as I want it, I am in the safest branch of service in the whole A. E. F. and not being a very sickly person I am usually in the best of health and enjoying life as much as I may. Evenings when we are in camp I generally play the banjo and Ralf Hagan our company clerk plays the lead on his mandolin and together we make quite a lot of noise and "Jazzy" music.

The last week or so has been quite encouraging hasn't it? We have been backing up the advance as usual and have gone up where things have happened very recently. We passed through country not entirely cleared of dead. The odour in places was quite sickening especially when we had to pass by dead horses and mules. I so one

PROF F.W. ROE
Assistant Dean
College of Letters & Science
University of WISCONSIN
ROBERT M. MARLING
CANDIDATE FOR
AVIATION CORPS

NO DATE

Typed Copy on Back-
July 31, 1918

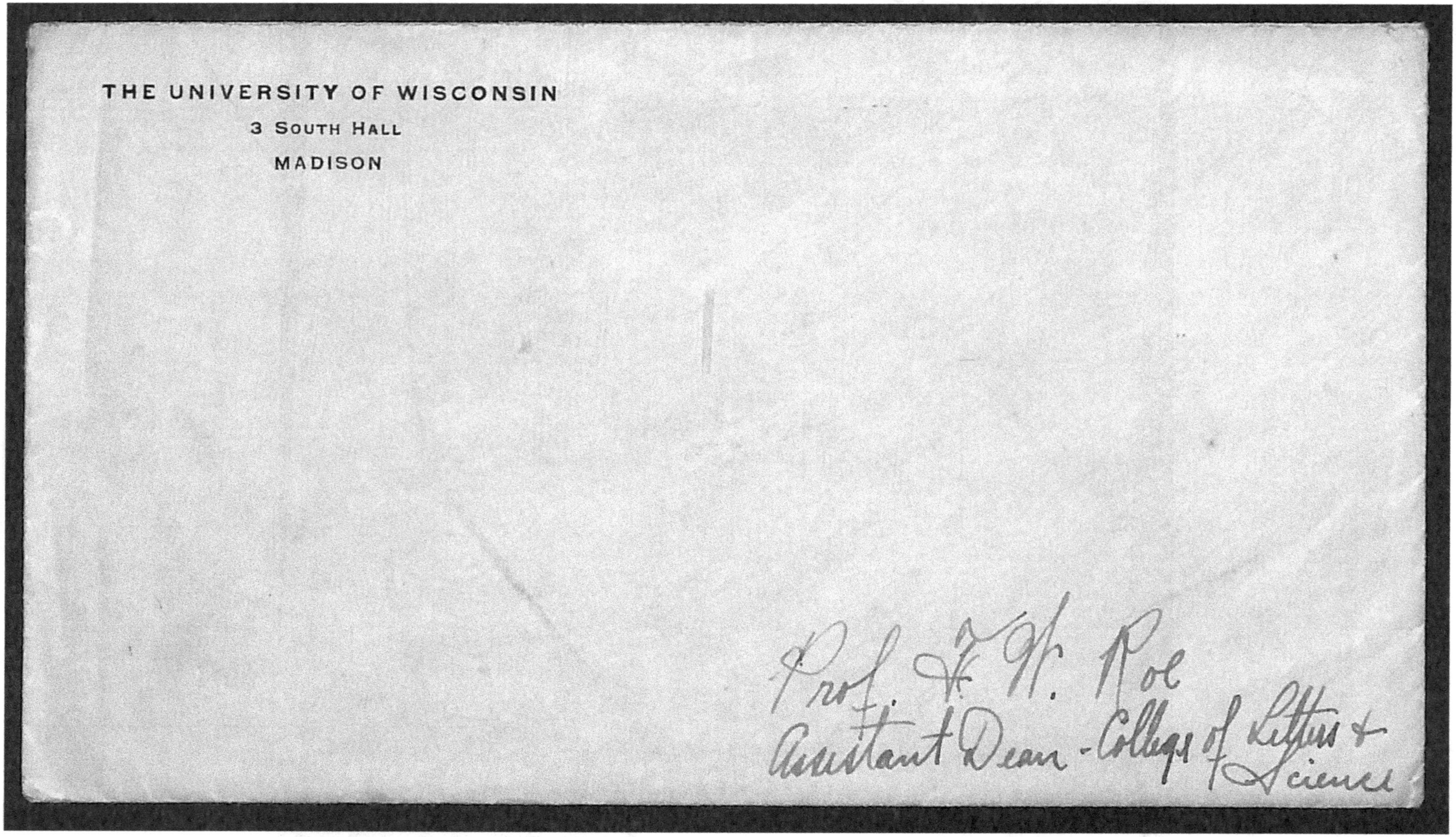
THE UNIVERSITY OF WISCONSIN
3 SOUTH HALL
MADISON

Prof. F. W. Roe
Assistant Dean - Colleges of Letters & Science

Mr. Robert Marling, who has been a student in the University of Wisconsin, has asked me to write a brief statement concerning his personal qualifications as a candidate for service in the ~~Ambulance~~ Aviation Corps.

I am very glad to say that Mr. Marling is a young man of unquestioned character. We who know him know that he will

be true and loyal to
every trust imposed upon
him. Whatever he pledges
himself too, he will do to
the utmost of his strength
and capacity. His habits, his
sense of integrity and loyalty,
his fine spirit of comradeship
and service to others, — these
qualities, I am confident,
will enable him to
render invaluable service
in the ~~Ambulance~~ Aviation Corps.
He will be found ready

to do his duty in full
measure and in the spirit
of devotion characteristic of
our best American manhood.

Mr. Marling, like so
many of our University boys,
is offering himself to the
service of the nation in
this time of emergency from
a high sense of patriotic
duty. I know that you
can depend upon him, for he
belongs to the class of our
most dependable young men.

F. W. Roe, Assistant Dean
May 20 - '17

Mr.Robert Marling, who has been a student in the University of Wisconsin, has asked me to write a brief statement concerning his personal qualifications as a candidate for service in the Aviation Corps.

Iam very glad to say that Mr.Marling is a young man of unquestionable character. We who know him know that he will be true and loyal to every trust imposed upon him. Whatever he pledges himself to do, he will do to the utmost of his strength and ability. His habits, his sense of ~~[illegible]~~ integrity and loyalty, his fine spirit of comradship and service to others,— these qualities, Iam confident, will make him to render invaluable service in the Aviation Corps. He will be found ready to do his duty in full measure and in the spirit of devotion characteristic of our best American manhood.

Mr.Marling like so many of our University boys, is offering himself to the of the nation in this time of emergency from a high sense of patriotic duty. I know that you can depend upon him, for he belongs to the class of our most dependable young men.

(signed)F.W.Roe.
Assistant Dean,
College of Letters & Science
University of Wisconsin.

Note:- Aviation substituted for Ambulance with Prof. Roe's permition.

R.N.M.

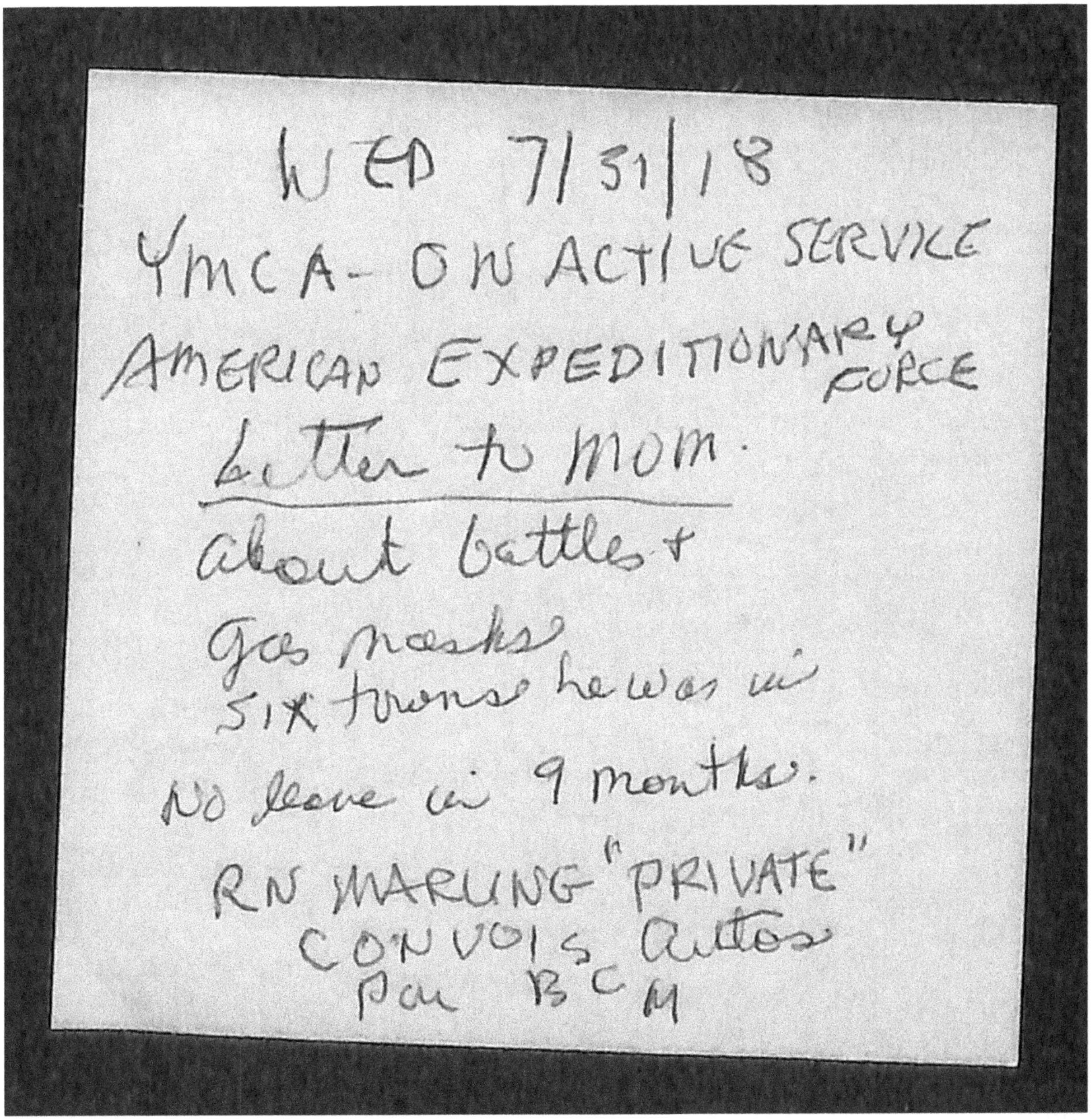

WED 7/31/18
YMCA- ON ACTIVE SERVICE
AMERICAN EXPEDITIONARY FORCE
Letter to Mom.

about battles &
gas masks
six towns he was in
No leave in 9 months.
RN MARLING "PRIVATE"
CONVOIS autos
par B C M

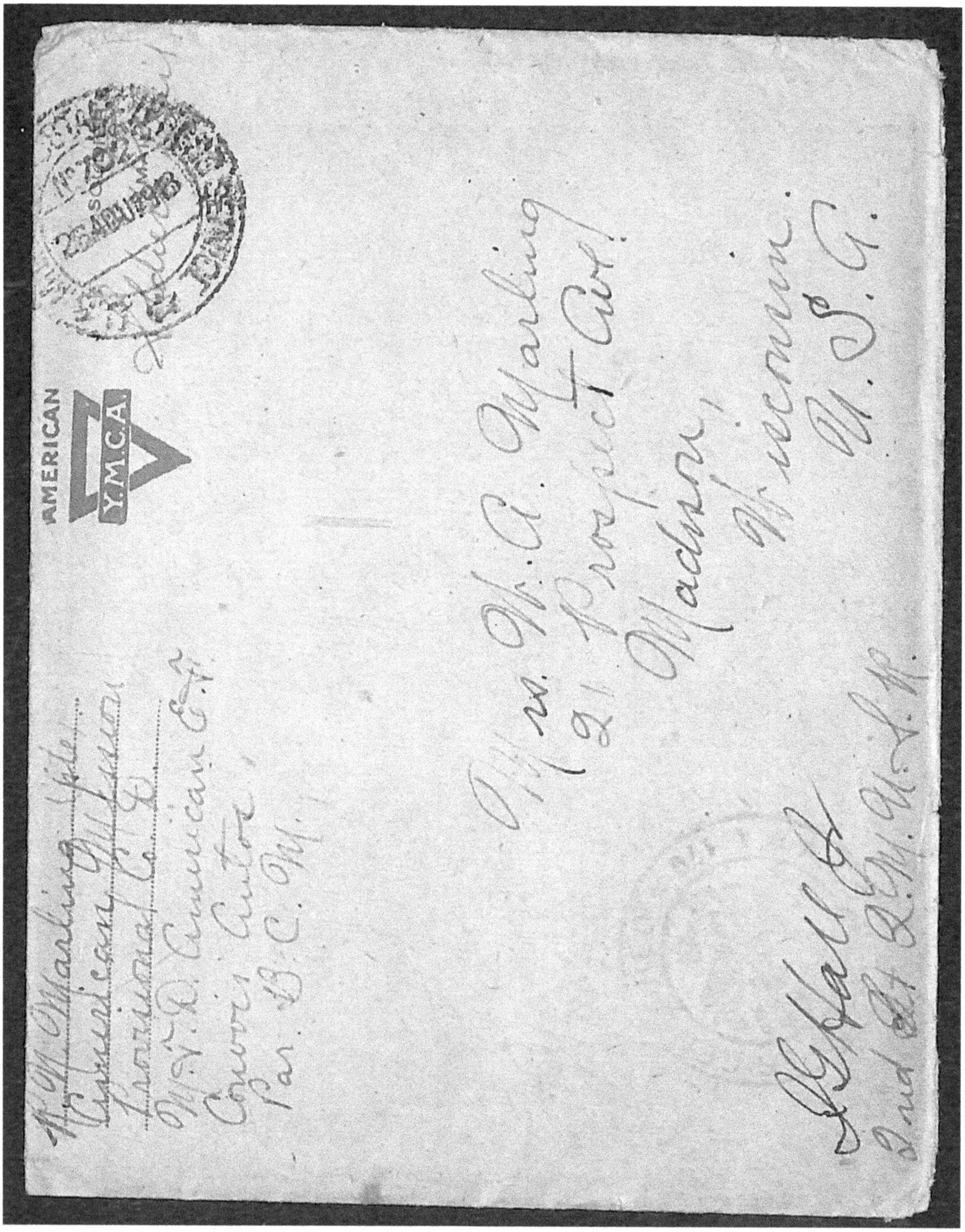
AMERICAN
Y.M.C.A.

R. N. Marling
American Mission
Provisional Co. D.
M.T.D. American E.F.
Co[illegible]tor
Par [illegible] M.

AMERICAN
Y.M.C.A.

ON ACTIVE SERVICE
WITH THE
AMERICAN EXPEDITIONARY FORCES

Wed. July 31st 1918

Dearest Mother,

I was very sorry to hear in your last letter that you missed Jimmie Vincent on his way thru Madison. I imagine that he too will be sorry not to have seen him. I was fortunate in seeing "Scary" Marshall the other day, but unfortunate in that I was alone on the truck and our truck train and his regiment of artillery were passing in opposite directions. I wanted very much to have a little chat with him as he was going up into action on the front east of the fifth town you mentioned, and I will probably not see him for

Dud Davis must have had quite a fall to be in the condition you say he is in. I hope that he will soon be fully recovered so that he can come back over here soon.

The little picture of Margaret was very good and shows how much she is changing. She will be quite a young lady when I come home. I haven't had that permission you asked about, but I hear they are coming soon and will anxiously await my turn. I hope that I can get to go with Sgt. Penniman and Sgt. Baker, for we have always been together on leaves in the states and we always some time. He saw me first and called out "Hello, Bob" to me and I just had time to answer with a "Hello Scary" before I passed by. He was looking fine and quite happy to be going into things it seemed. I got quite a laugh out of his outfit. The all had there gas masks out ready to dive into them and they were still miles from the front and I had just come from up there—fairly close. Several of the boys noticed a little gas up there—their noses were tickling and eyes smarting and running. "Scary's" regiment must have had an alert for the certainly were all set for it.

I am glad to hear that Charles Moore is recovering so nicely and hope he will soon the flying again and making a name for himself. He certainly is a lucky fellow to be in that service, I certainly envy him. I'd give anything to be where he is now. I think I could have been if I were not in such a hurry to get over here. Charles' eyes were no better than mine and I think I could have passed as well as he did. I've found that it doesn't pay to be so impulsive. I regretted it in the Ambulance Co. and I regret it now. The steadier fellows in my old outfit who stayed at Camp Sherman finally got into aviation and as I had my application in with them I undoubtedly would have been called at the same time they were

AMERICAN Y.M.C.A.

ON ACTIVE SERVICE
WITH THE
AMERICAN EXPEDITIONARY FORCES

.... 191....

have a fine time together. Jimmie Baker is now at an officers training school, and ought to return soon. When he does we will have to try to arrange to get our permissions the same week. I haven't had a leave since the last of October - nine months - and that leave only for five days - closer to six when I got back.

I was at the second town you mentioned just a few hours before it fell into the hands of the boche. That was quite an exciting night for all of us. The third is the site of our old camp, and it was there that

I was forced to believe that there was a war going on. I been in the first six towns you mentioned on one or another of our many trips. I am now behind the front around where I saw "Scary". You will learn the details of my whereabouts when we see or write Fred Hummel when he arrives home, which will be before this letter reaches you.

Hasn't the latest allied push been a wonder? Our fellows are going into it like veterans and equaling the fine record of the picked shock troops of France. Germany won't be able to stop them at all when we have them here in sufficient numbers, which will be soon at the rate they are now coming

My deepest love and devotion to all of the dear ones and most of all to you, dear.

Bob.

AUGUST 16, 1918

Dear Father

1st day not rolling for weeks

TRUCK IS IN SHOP

FOR REPAIRS

driving over late

Battlefields

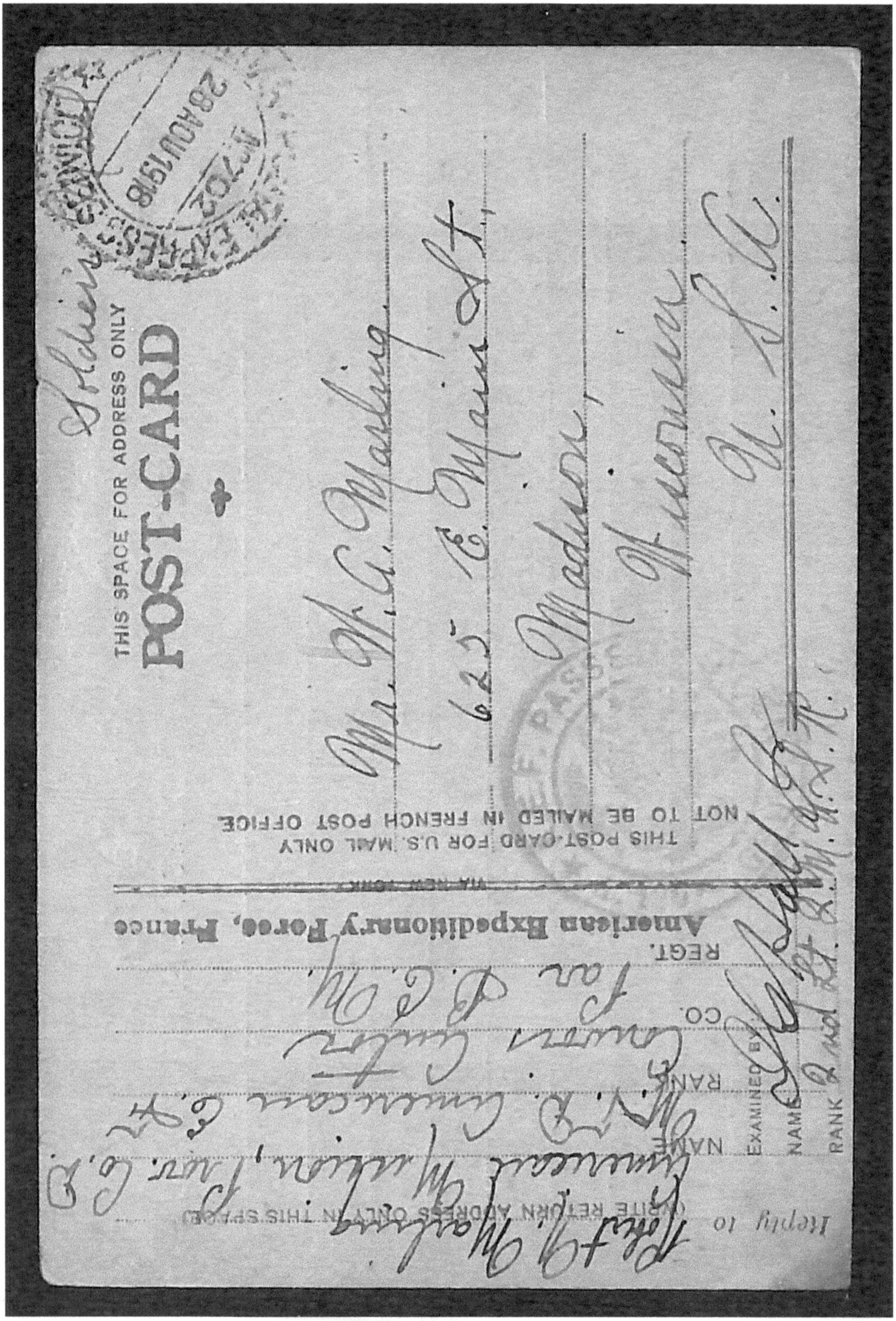
THIS SPACE FOR ADDRESS ONLY

POST-CARD

THIS POST-CARD FOR U.S. MAIL ONLY

NOT TO BE MAILED IN FRENCH POST OFFICE

American Expeditionary Force, France

VIA NEW YORK

Reply to

(WRITE RETURN ADDRESS ONLY IN THIS SPACE)

NAME

RANK

CO.

REGT.

EXAMINED BY:

NAME

RANK

28 AOU 1918

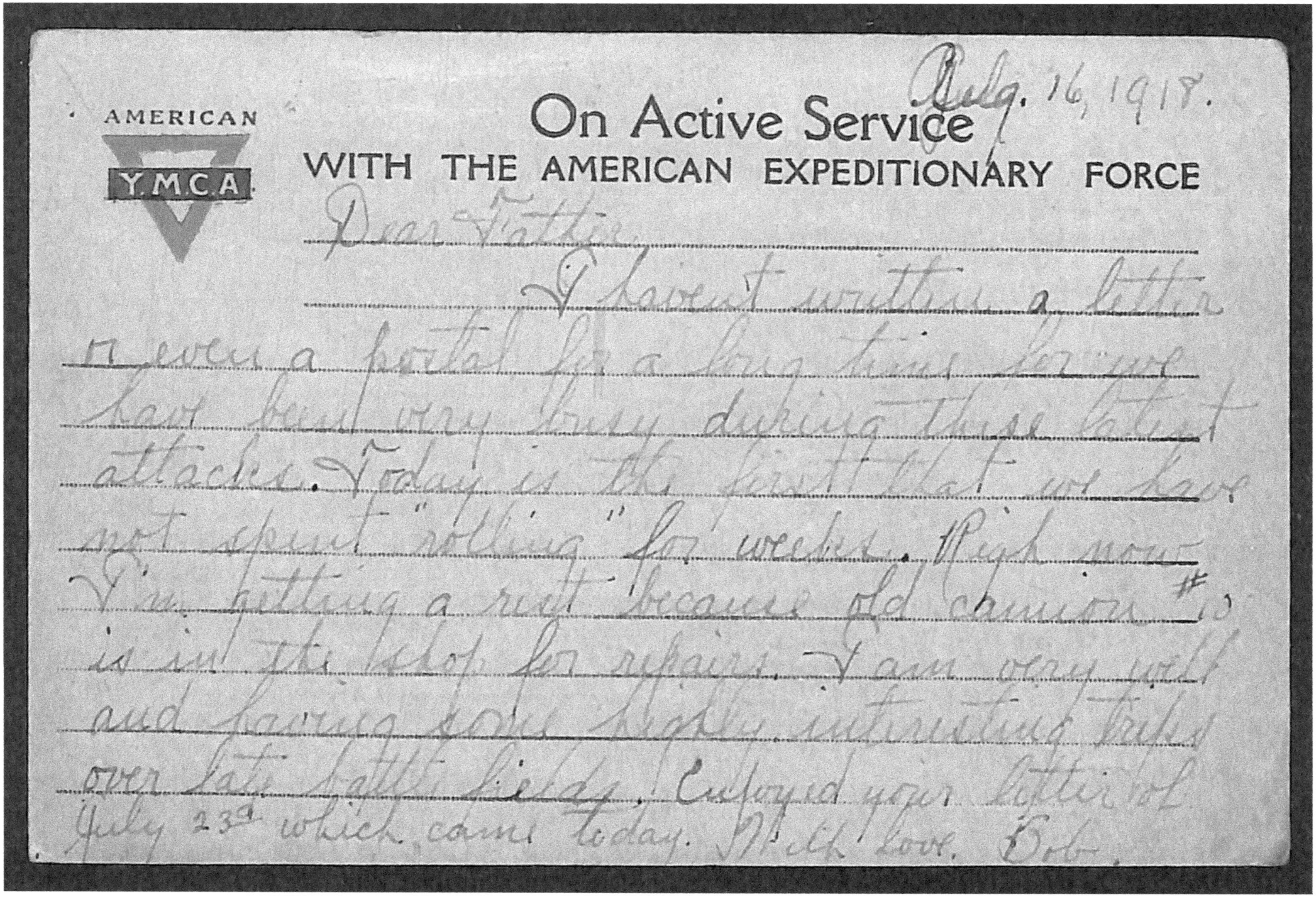
AMERICAN Y.M.C.A.

On Active Service

WITH THE AMERICAN EXPEDITIONARY FORCE

Aug. 16, 1918.

Dear Father,

I haven't written a letter or even a postal for a long time for we have been very busy during these latest attacks. Today is the first that we have not spent "rolling" for weeks. Right now I'm getting a rest because old camion #10 is in the shop for repairs. I am very well and having some highly interesting trips over late battle fields. Enjoyed your letter of July 23rd which came today. With love, Bob.

AUGUST 16, 2018
POST CARD YMCA
got letter from July 4, 8,
12 + 18 & 22nd.

Can only work -
eat & sleep.
their constant service
has helped late successes
Reserve has been
congratulated

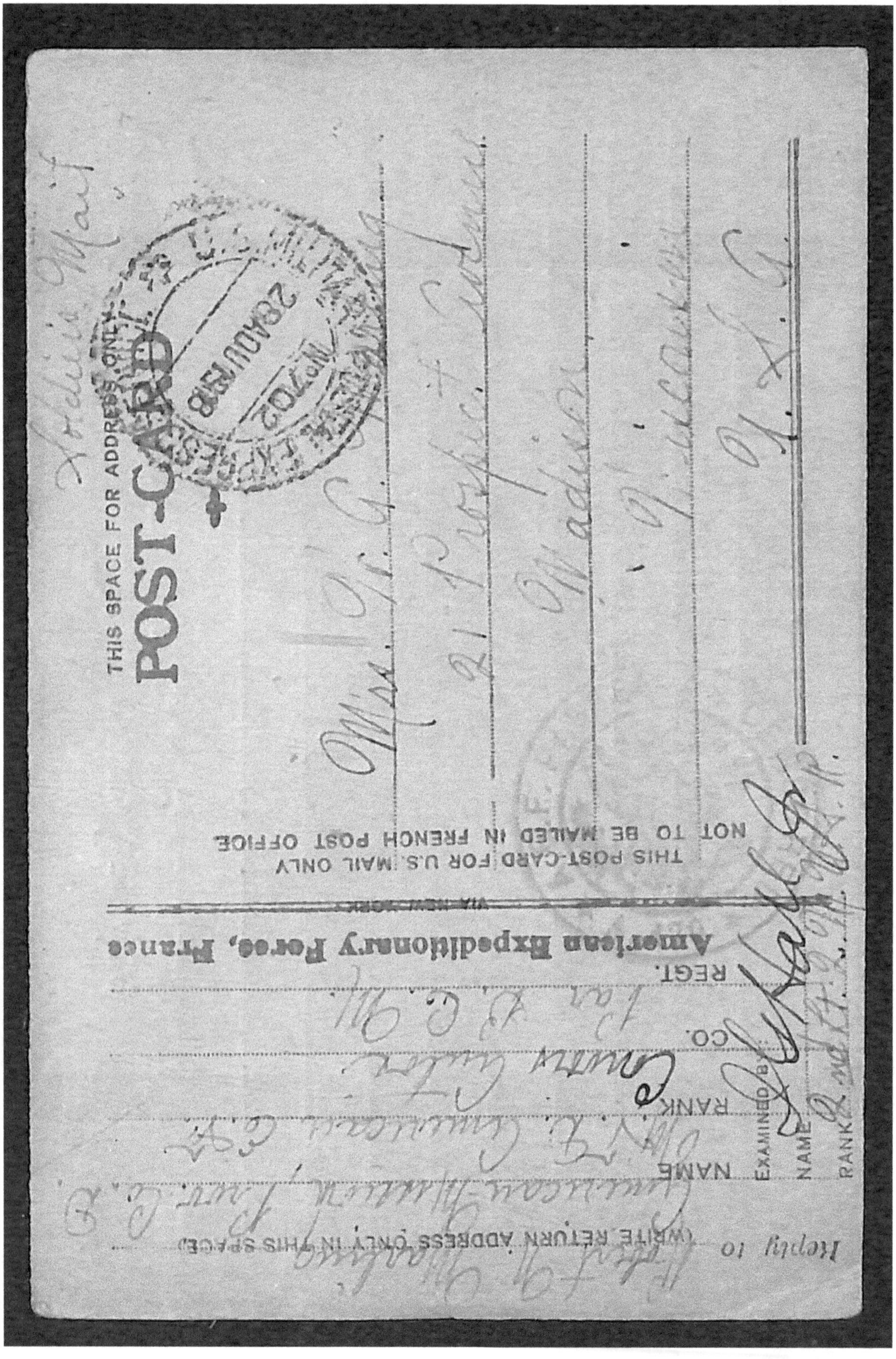
THIS SPACE FOR ADDRESS ONLY
POST-CARD
Soldier's Mail
28 AOUT 18
21 Prospect
Madison
Wisconsin
U.S.A.
THIS POST-CARD FOR U.S. MAIL ONLY
NOT TO BE MAILED IN FRENCH POST OFFICE
VIA NEW YORK
American Expeditionary Force, France
REGT.
CO.
RANK
NAME
EXAMINED BY:
NAME
RANK
Reply to (WRITE RETURN ADDRESS ONLY IN THIS SPACE)

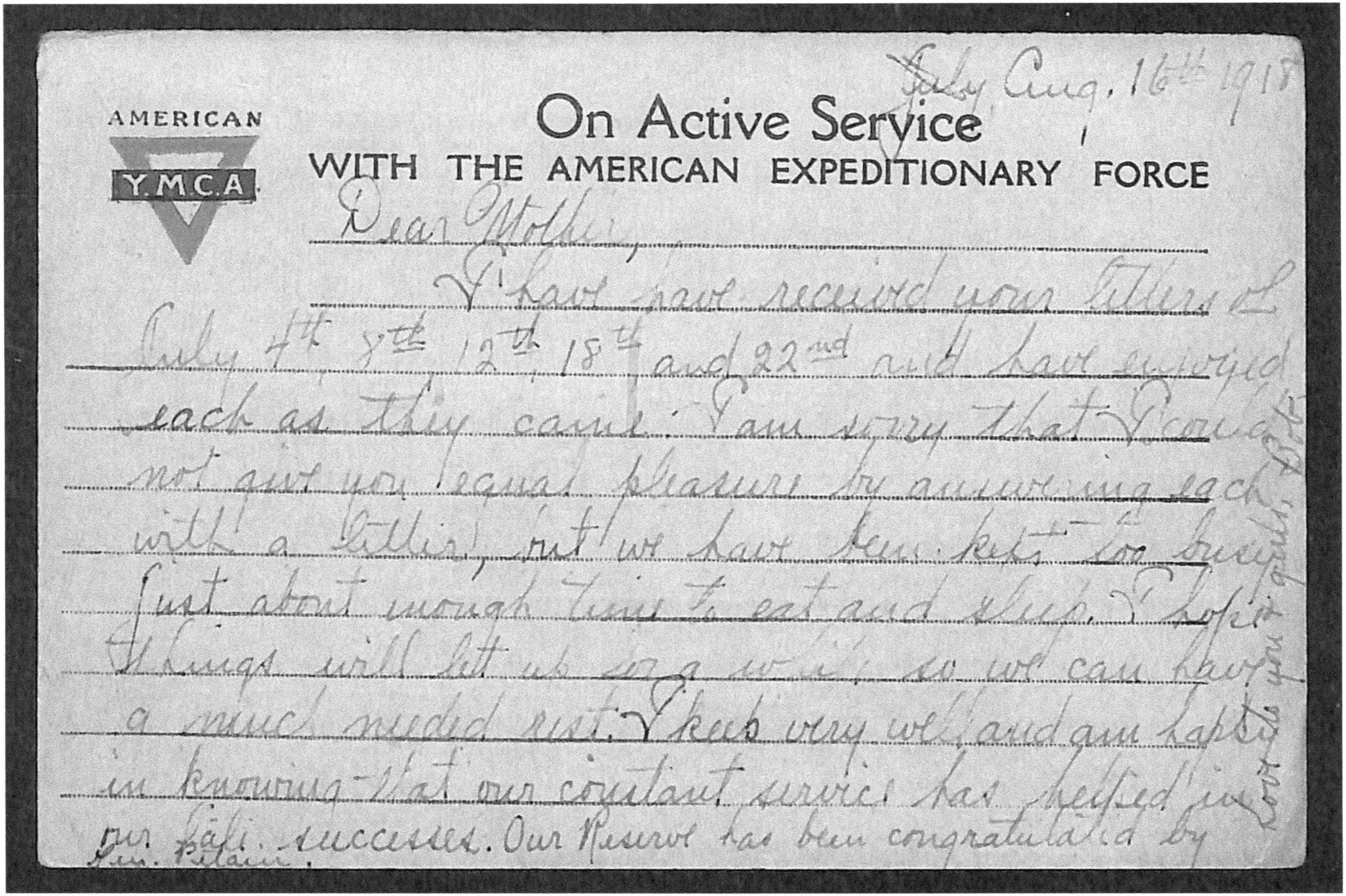

AMERICAN Y.M.C.A

On Active Service
WITH THE AMERICAN EXPEDITIONARY FORCE

~~July~~ Aug. 16th 1918

Dear Mother,

I have have received your letters of July 4th, 8th, 12th, 18th and 22nd and have enjoyed each as they came. I am sorry that I could not give you equal pleasure by answering each with a letter, but we have been kept too busy just about enough time to eat and sleep. I hope things will let up for a while, so we can have a much needed rest. I keep very well and am happy in knowing that our constant service has helped in our late successes. Our Reserve has been congratulated by Gen. Petain.

Love to you, papa, Ed.

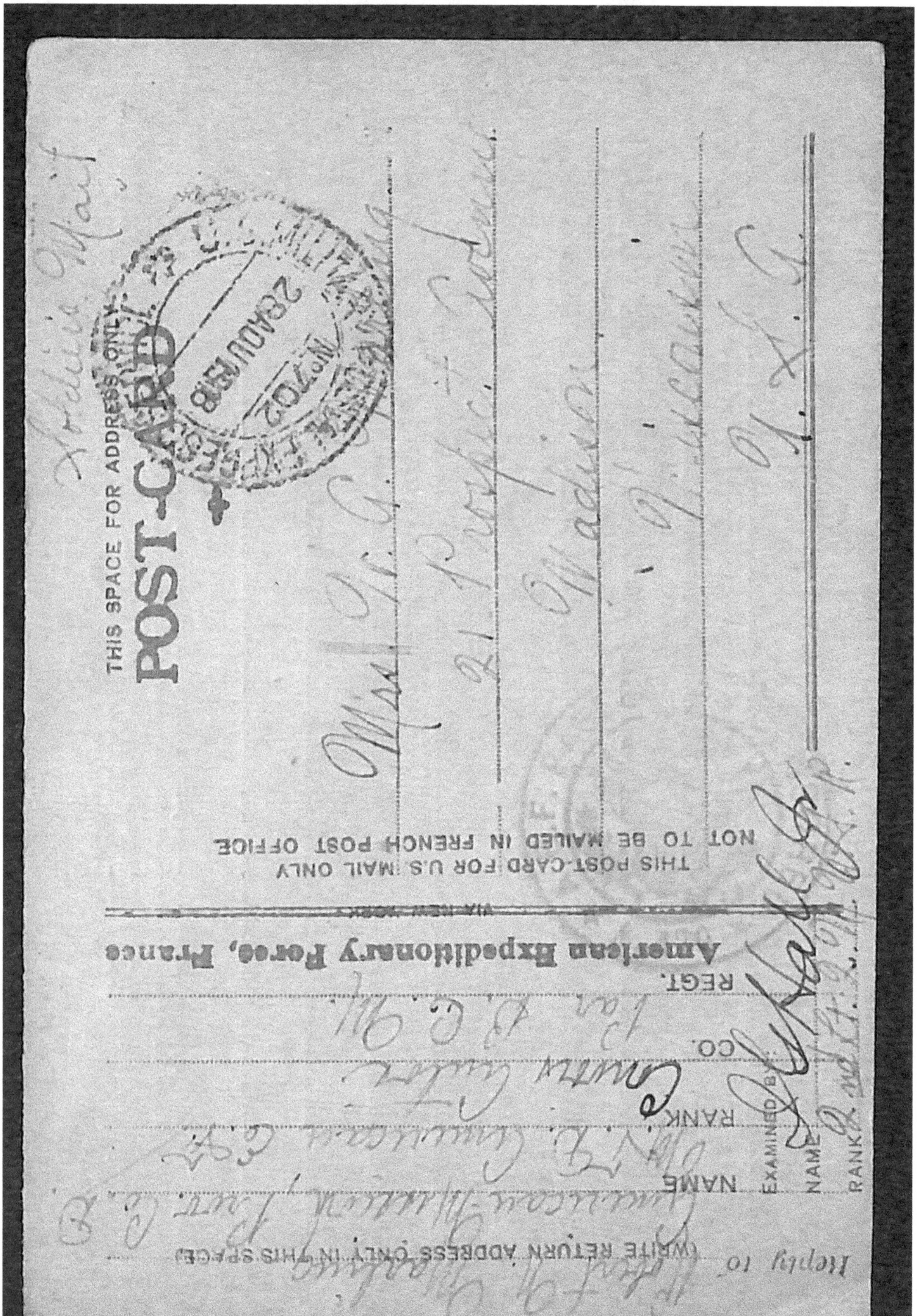

THIS SPACE FOR ADDRESS ONLY

POST-CARD

THIS POST-CARD FOR U.S. MAIL ONLY

NOT TO BE MAILED IN FRENCH POST OFFICE

American Expeditionary Force, France

REGT.

CO.

RANK

NAME

EXAMINED BY:

NAME

RANK

(WRITE RETURN ADDRESS ONLY IN THIS SPACE)

Reply to

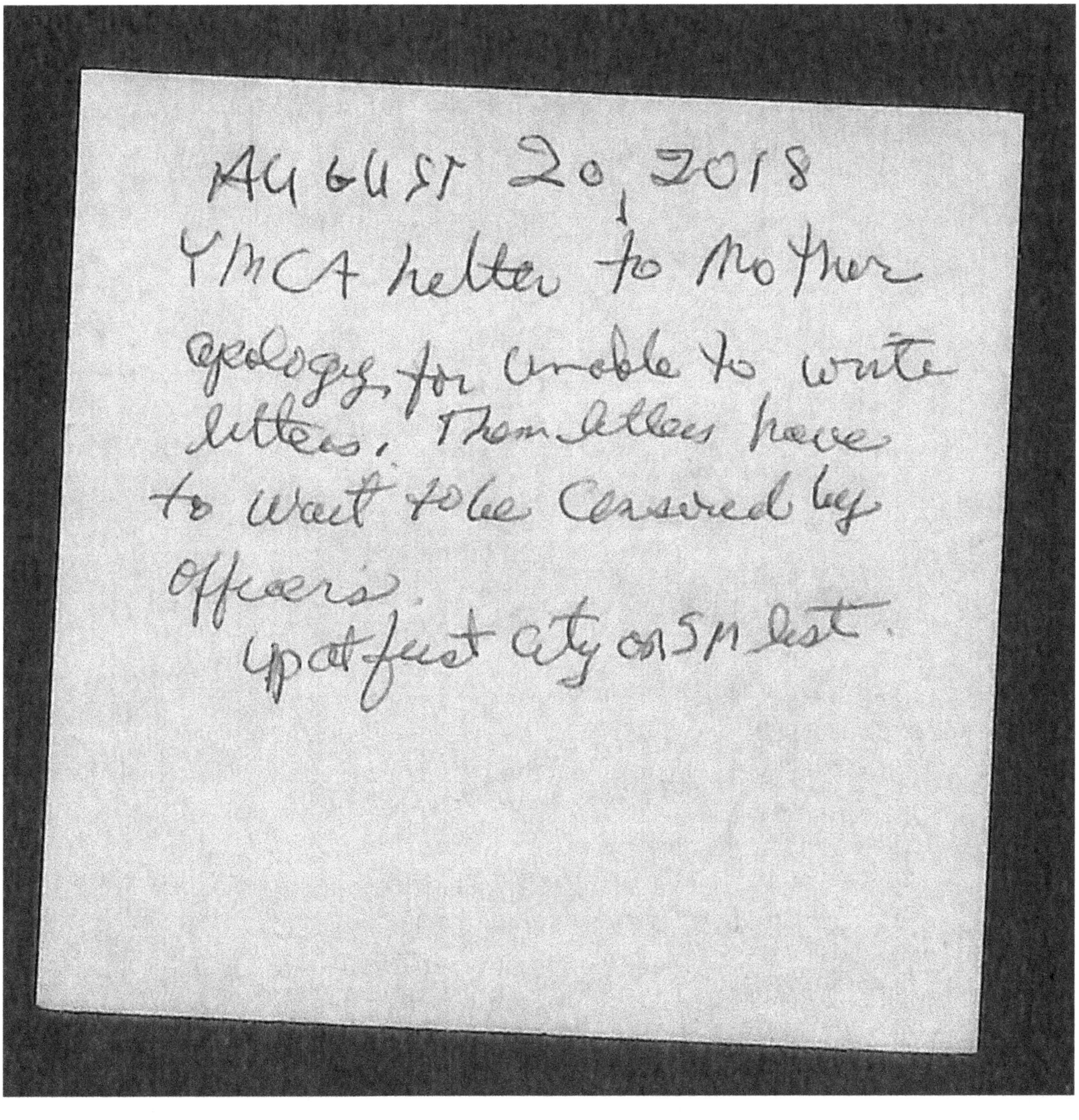
AUGUST 20, 2018
YMCA letter to Mother
apology, for unable to write
letters. Them letters have
to wait to be censored by
officers.
up at first city on SM list.

AMERICAN
Y.M.C.A.

Pt. R. N. Marling
American Mission
M.T.D. American E.F.
Convois Autos
Par B.C.M.

AMERICAN Y.M.C.A.

ON ACTIVE SERVICE
WITH THE
AMERICAN EXPEDITIONARY FORCE

Aug. 20th 1918

Dear Mother,

I am very sorry that I have been unable to write a letter to you for some time for I know how you feel when no letter comes for weeks on end. I wrote a card the other day and hope it reaches you for I don't know if this letter will go thru now or whether it will be delayed. Our lieut. is now on his permission so unless one of the other officers in our groupe will censor this, it will not be on its way to you for some time.

For about two weeks or more we have been up near the first city on your list and have been serving the armies up here

hurt. The other Ray Harris had his left leg run over by a truck. I think I told you about Ray and another letter and said that they would have to amputate. Later they decided that the leg could be saved. I certainly hope so.

Tell the girls that I will write to them when I have time and in the meantime I would like very much to hear from them. Margaret and Cecilia are certainly able to write very nice letters and Eleanor's are very interesting and entertaining. I've laughted a great deal over the last one.

Beaucoup love for all of you,
Your
Bob.

continually. No one has had time to rest for we are either out on a convoy or else we are working on the trucks to put them in shape for another day or week of "rolling". Some weeks we have barely time to eat and sleep, with no time to clean and grease the joints on the car ecept that few moments we have while loading or unloading.

I thought that the front on which we last served was badly shelled, but up here I have come to ~~[illegible]~~ know what absolute demolition of towns means. They tell me that it is the American artillery that has done most of it and if it is true, I hope they soon have a chance to perfect themselves firing on German towns. One town up here must have had at least ten shells hit each house for nothing stood except wrecks of churches and government buildings of the most massive construction.

I thought that I had told you that I hurt my hand on the camion. I jumped out over the tail-gate and tore my palm open on the head of a screw that was sticking out. It also caught under my ring and ripped it off together with a couple square inches of hide. Yes, thank you, it is entirely healed now. Two of my old friends (of Ambulance Co. No 9.) who came over in the 108th with me have been hurt. One, our old cook, was hit in the back of the head with a piece of a bomb, but is not dangerously

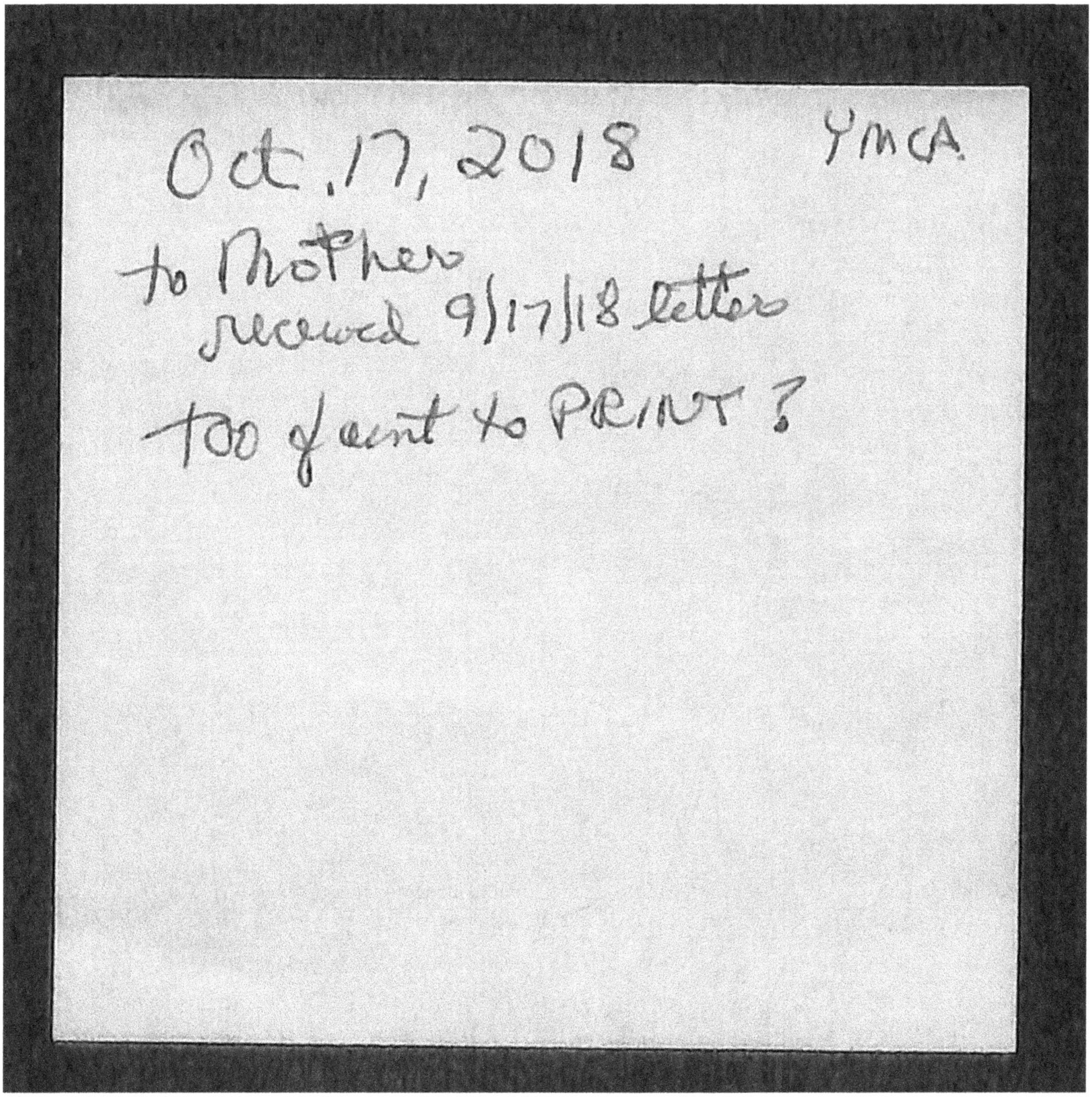
Oct. 17, 2018 YMCA

to Mother
received 9/17/18 letter

Too faint to PRINT?

PASSED AS CENSORED

AMERICAN Y.M.C.A.

ON ACTIVE SERVICE
WITH THE
AMERICAN EXPEDITIONARY FORCES

Oct. 17, 1918

Dearest Mother,

I have received your [illegible]

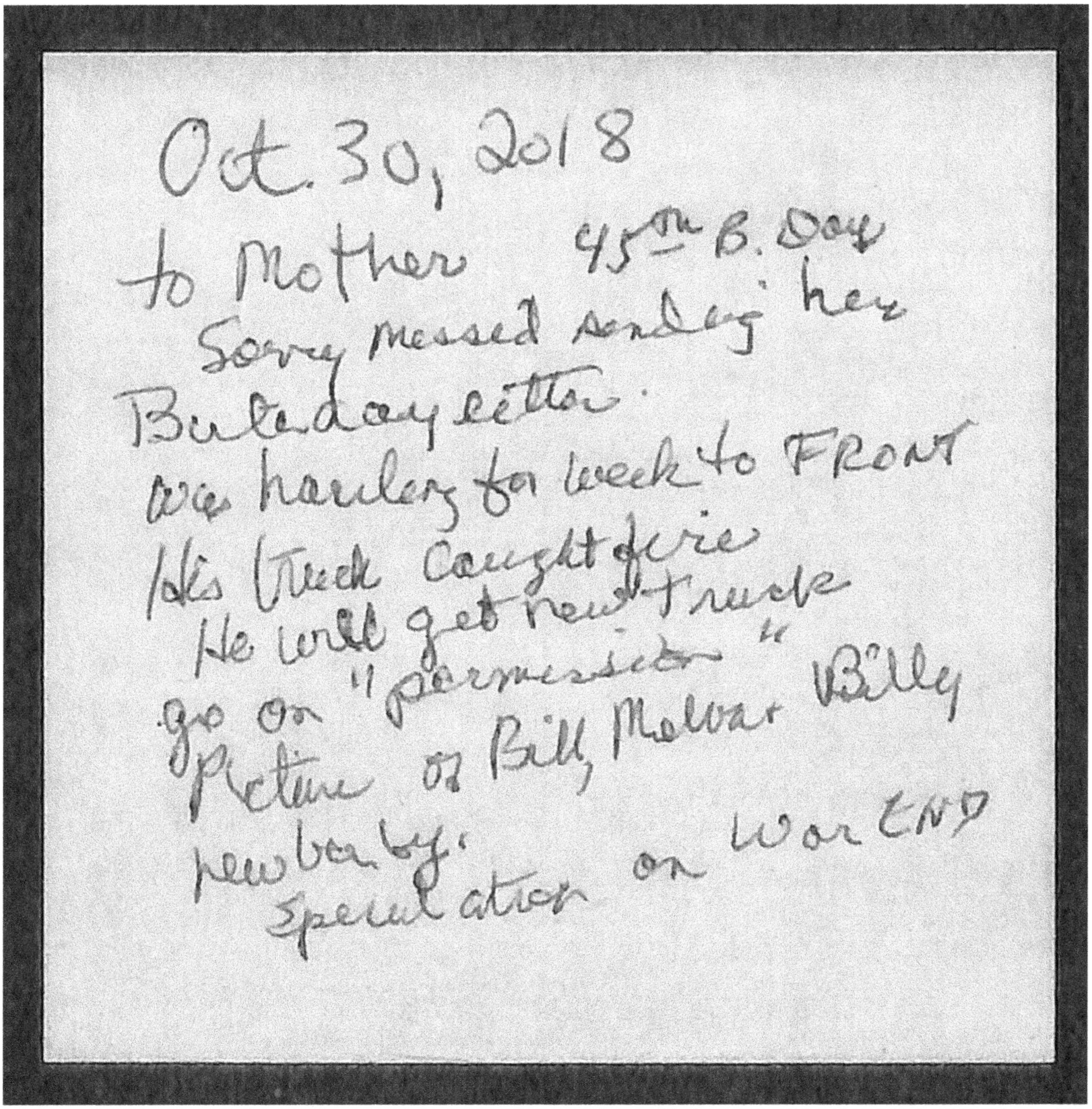

Oct. 30, 2018

to Mother 45th B. Day

Sorry missed sending her

Birthday letter.

was hauling for week to FRONT

His truck caught fire

He will get new truck

go on "permission"

Picture of Bill, Melva + Billy

new baby.

Speculation on War END

AMERICAN
Y.M.C.A.
SOLDIER'S MAIL
Soldier's Mail
BORDEAUX
1918
Mrs. W. A. Marling
21 Prospect Avenue
Madison,
Wisconsin
U.S.A.

P.M. Marling
American Mission E.F.
M.T.D. American C.P.
Provisional Autos
B.C.M.

AMERICAN Y.M.C.A. ON ACTIVE SERVICE WITH THE AMERICAN EXPEDITIONARY FORCES

Oct. 30th 1918.

Kel
R.J. MTS

Dear Mother,

I'm very sorry that I was unable to write a letter to you on your birthday, but it so happened that I had to make a pretty long trip that took me out early and brought me back late at night. I have been away from camp for about a week; the first few days hauling — up to the front. On one of these trips my truck caught fire, and I had to take it to the Independent Atelier and later to a division park. They tell me that I am to get a new truck for it. I certainly hope so. The 1st Independent Atelier is in the same town with

About all we hear now-a-days is "How soon do you think the war will be over?" Most every one seems to think it a matter of days, or at most a month, and nearly all set the date as some-time before Christmas, while a few calamity howlers insist on next spring. Already Austria is clamoring for peace, and Germany is "willing to discuss conditions on which a peace may be accepted"; I still rather expect that wait till the Allies pound her lines a little longer and then we'll be a change of tune, — something like unconditional surrender. Let us hope so!

Much love to you and congratulations on your forty-fifth (?) birthday, love to Dad and the girls,

Your affectionate son, Bob

my old outfit, the 408th and consequently I had a pretty fine time the few days I was over there. The sergeant in charge told me, after the first day, to make myself scarce as there was no work for me to do. Consequently I spent most of my time with my old friends Henry Campbell, Jim Baker, Lawrence Penniman (all top sergeants) and Sergeants Brown, Hickey, Dawson, Shaw, McGregor and others. I stayed with Henry Campbell and he appointed me his "adjutant". I filled the job so well that he insists that I transfer back to the old bunch again. I certainly am tempted to do it – after I go on my permission.

I have had several chances to go – alone – but I signed up to go with Sergt Wright and so have waited for him. We were to start in about two days, but just now there is another sergeant away and consequently Whit Wright is needed here.

I wrote a letter to you yesterday, but being away from camp I had to carry it with me. This afternoon I came back, and this evening decided to rewrite the letter because I found your letter of Oct. 3d waiting for me. It contained the pictures of Bill, Melo, and Billy Jo. They certainly are fine, thanks you very much for sending them. Bill's smile in one of them is a dead giveaway. You can see "proud father" written all over his face, and why not? for "Billy-Bob" is "some kid".

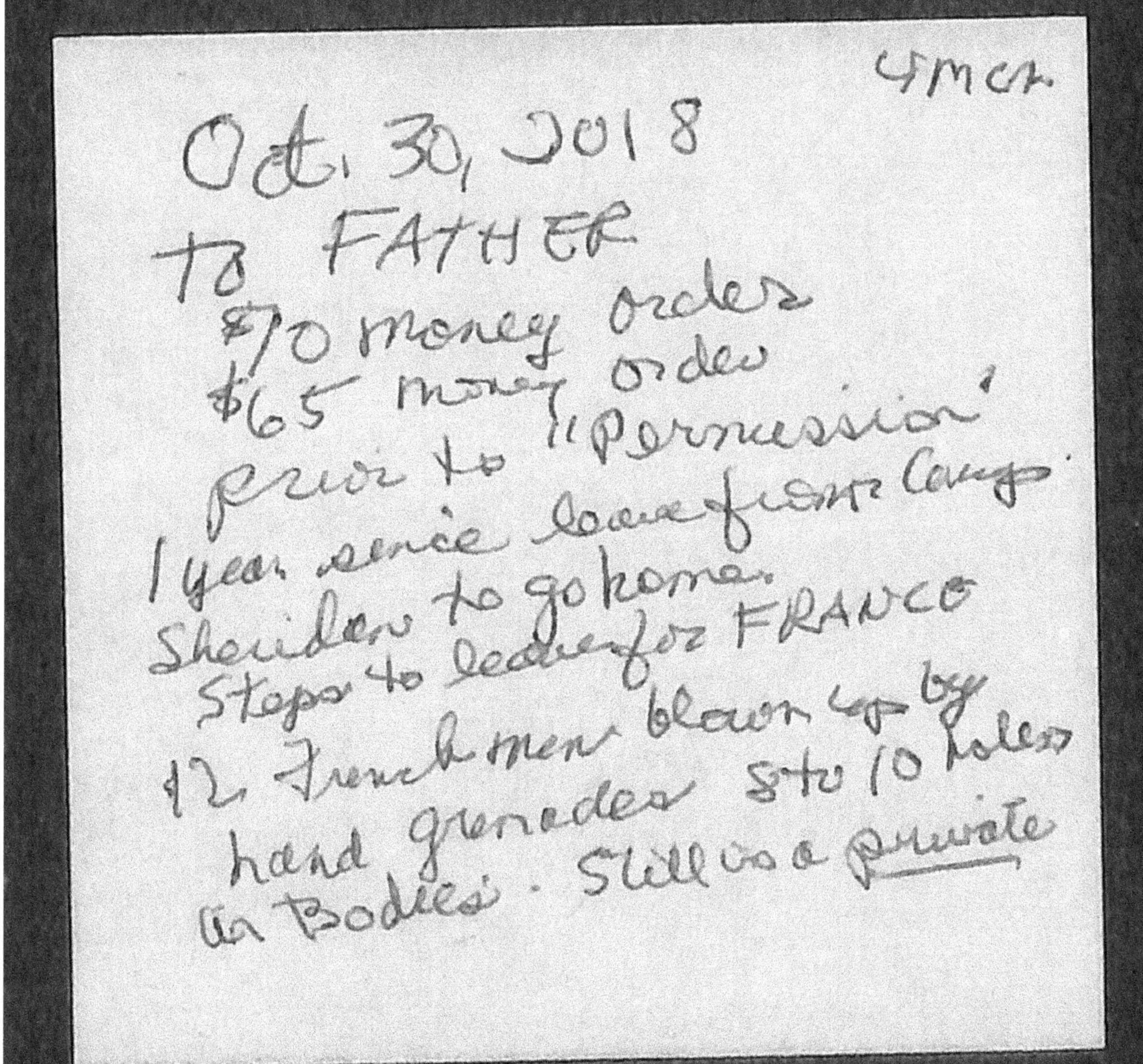

YMCA

Oct. 30, 1918

To FATHER

$70 money order

$65 money order

prior to "permission"

1 year since leave from Camp.

Sheridan to go home.

Steps to leave for FRANCE

12 Frenchmen blown up by

hand grenades 8 to 10 holes

in Bodies. Still is a private

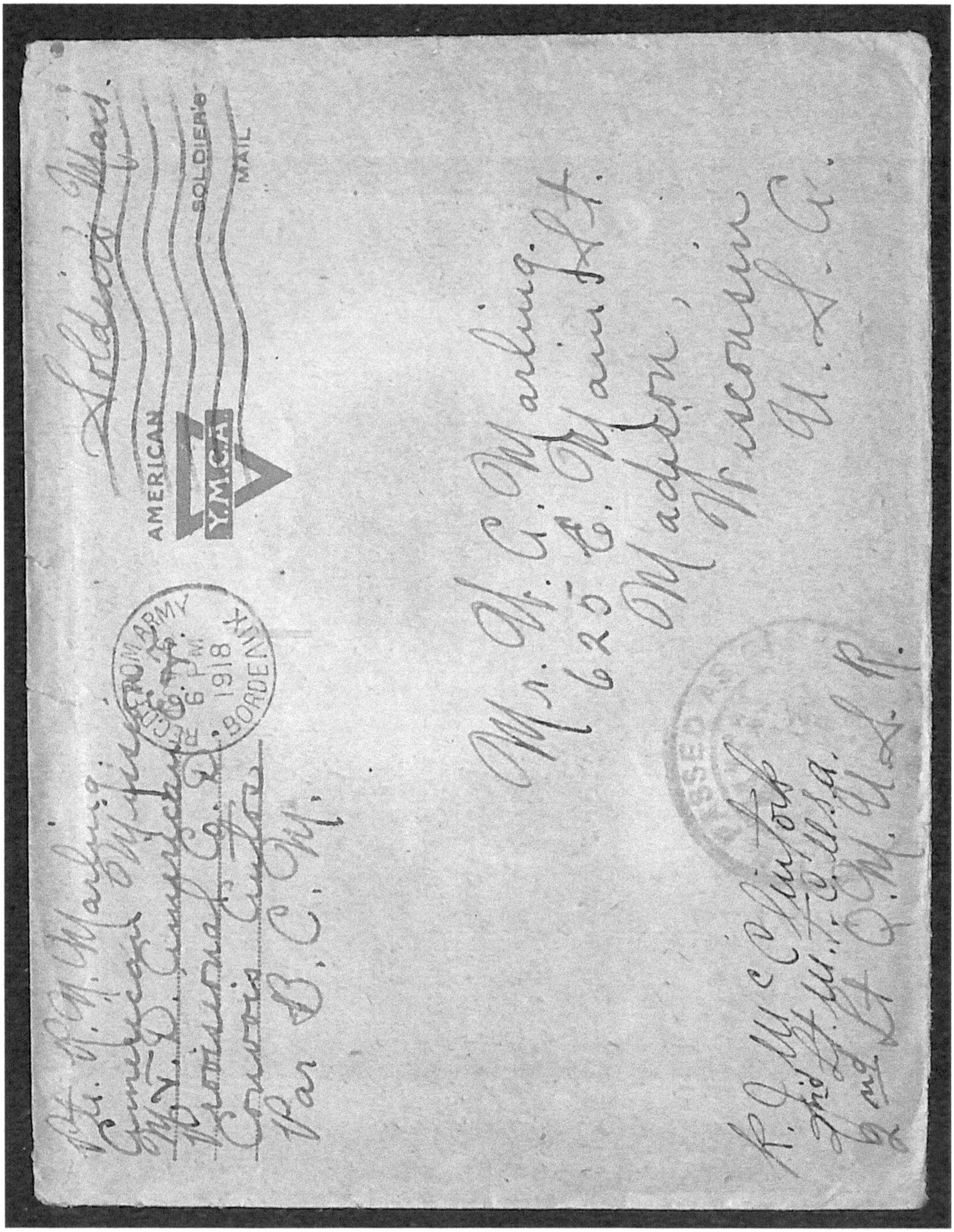
AMERICAN
Y.M.C.A.
SOLDIER'S MAIL
1918

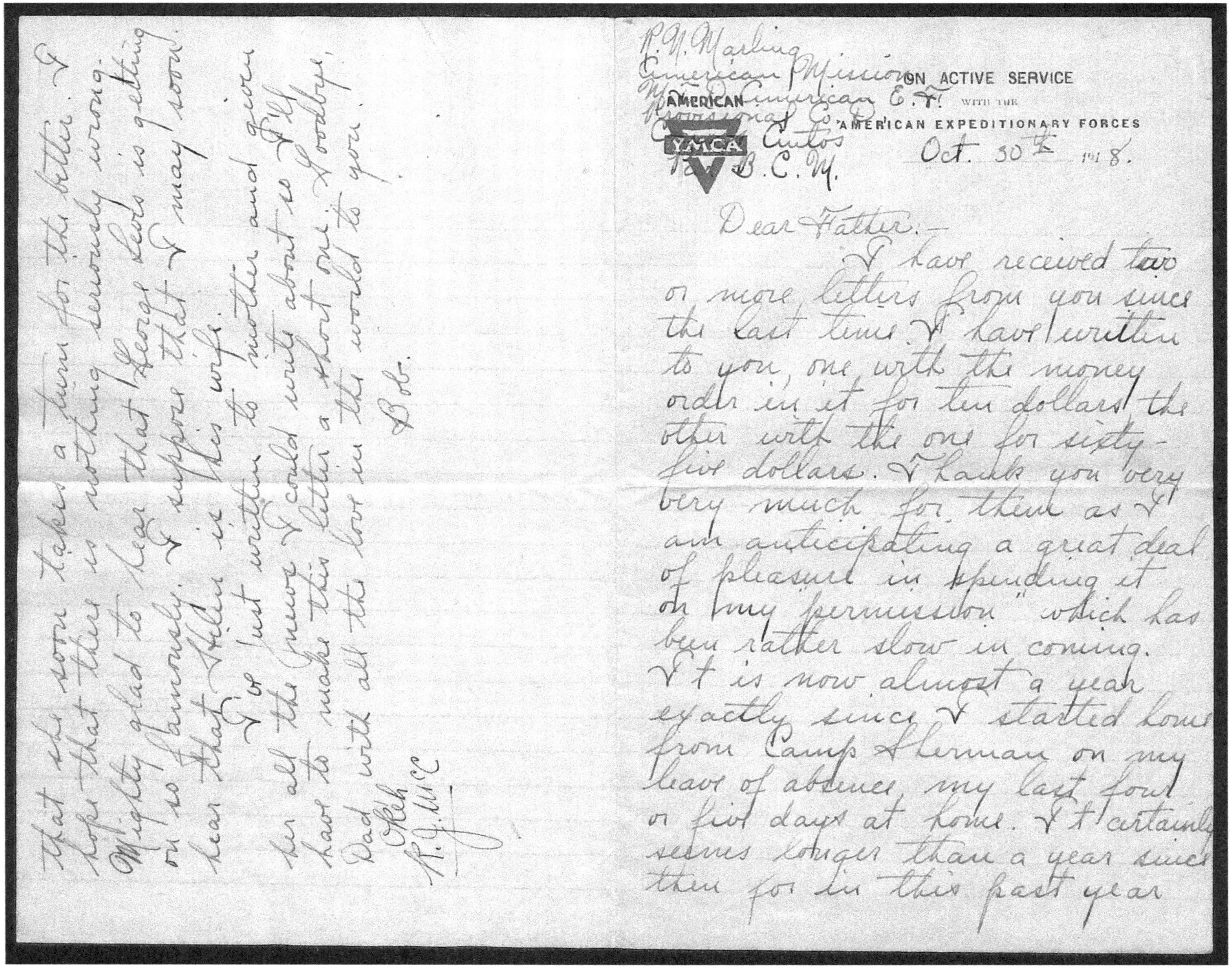

R. N. Marling
American Mission
M. D. American E. F.
Provisional Co. D
Autos
B. C. M.

AMERICAN Y.M.C.A. ON ACTIVE SERVICE WITH THE AMERICAN EXPEDITIONARY FORCES

Oct. 30th 1918.

Dear Father:—

I have received two or more letters from you since the last time I have written to you, one with the money order in it for ten dollars the other with the one for sixty-five dollars. I thank you very very much for them as I am anticipating a great deal of pleasure in spending it on my "permission" which has been rather slow in coming. It is now almost a year exactly since I started home from Camp Sherman on my leave of absence, my last four or five days at home. It certainly seems longer than a year since then for in this past year

that she soon takes a turn for the better. I hope that there is nothing seriously wrong. Mighty glad to hear that George Lewis is getting on so famously. I suppose that I may soon hear that Helen is his wife.

I've just written to mother and given her all the news I could write about so I'll have to make this letter a short one. Goodbye, Dad with all the love in the world to you.

Bob.

R. J. McC

so much has happened to me. First was our leave-taking at the hotel in Chilicothe, then the trip to Camp Merritt and our long quarantine there, after which came the long trip across the water and my first impressions of France. My first impressions have been lasting for I still think France the most beautiful and picturesque country I have seen. For the most part I like the people who seem very kind and sympathetic and so genuine. They have made us feel at home wherever we have gone, and now that we are in newly retaken territory we miss them very much!

The other day my training, that I received in the old ambulance company, stood me in pretty good stead. Twelve Frenchmen were pretty badly blown up by five or more hand grenades and I happened to hear the explosions and be there among the first and helped carry the men in off the road and help in bandaging. Some poor fellows had eight or ten ugly holes in them while most of the others had from four to six wounds.

Don't bother about underwear as I have now had an issue and it is pretty good stuff, quite good enough for any private in Uncle Sam's army. I get the State Journal quite regularly so please keep on sending it as it keeps me posted on what is going on at home.

I'm very sorry to hear that grandmother is not recovering very well after her fall, and hope

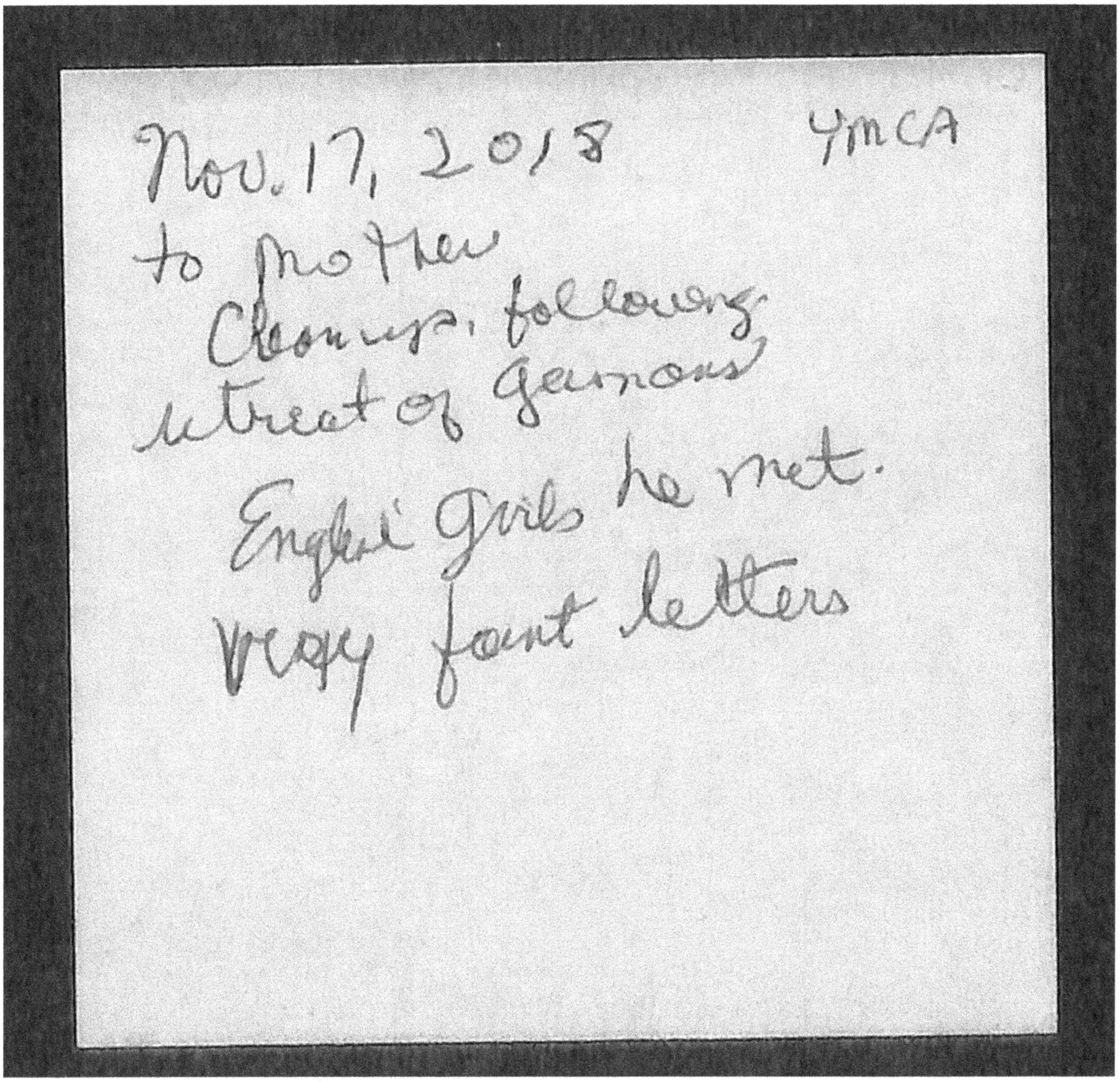

Nov. 17, 2018 YMCA
to mother
Cleanup, following
retreat of Germans
English Girls he met.
very faint letters

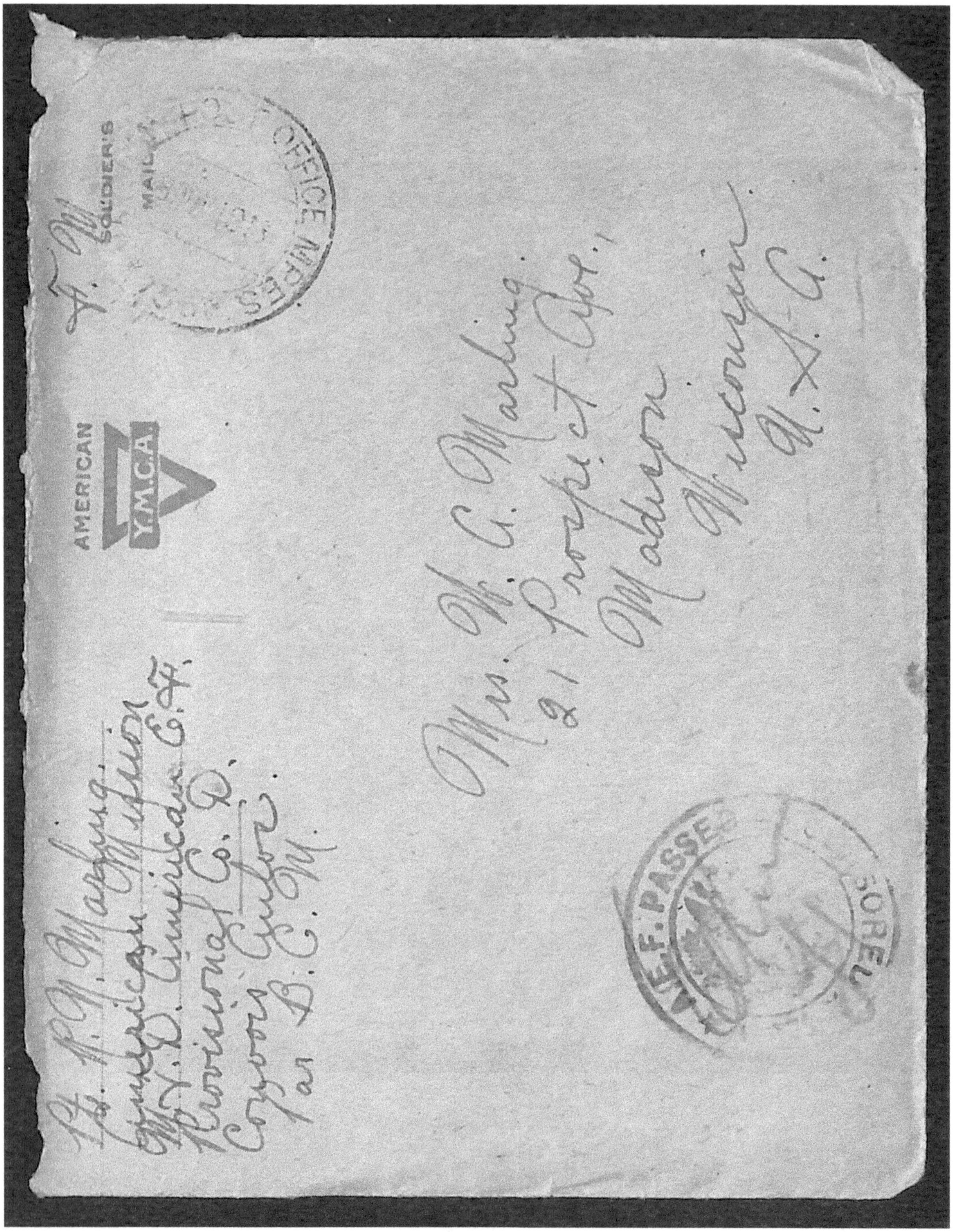
AMERICAN
Y.M.C.A.
SOLDIER'S MAIL

ON ACTIVE SERVICE
WITH THE
AMERICAN EXPEDITIONARY FORCE
Y.M.C.A.
191

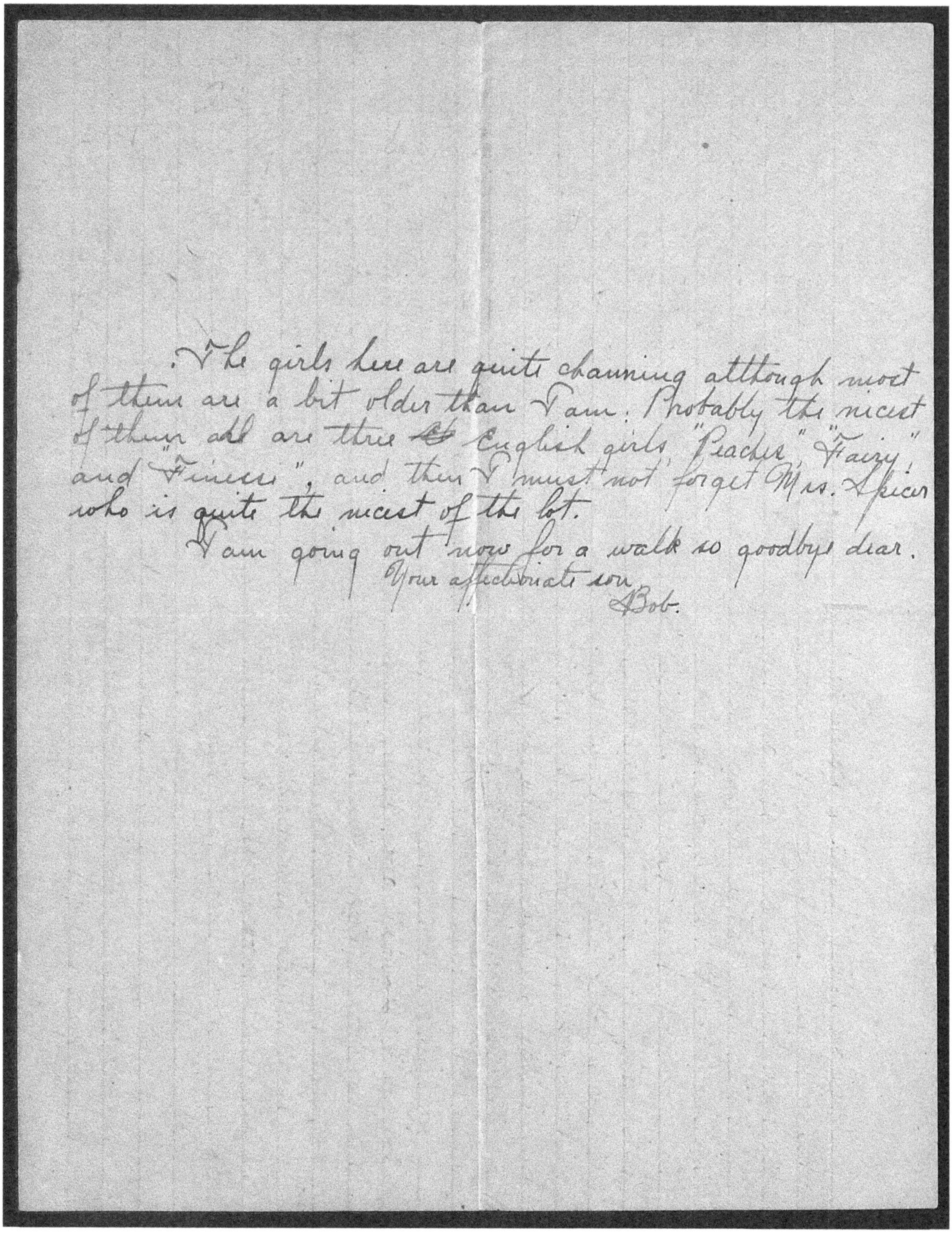

The girls here are quite charming although most of them are a bit older than I am. Probably the nicest of them all are three ~~E~~ English girls, "Peaches" "Fairy," and "Finesse", and then I must not forget Mrs. Spicer who is quite the nicest of the lot.

I am going out now for a walk so goodbye dear.

Your affectionate son
Bob.

AMERICAN
Y.M.C.A.
ARMY M.P.E.S.
1918
NOV 25
5 PM
702
U.S.
A.E.F.

Nov. 21, 1918

Dear Dad.

FIRST Furlough

package from Marshall Fields

Batch of Cooties

4 girls treated him like a prince

Climbed to see Mt. Blanc.

"Tea party, violin concert, picnic

first taste of freedom

day after Armistice in Paris

in AIX - Sleeping

AFTER WAR OVER

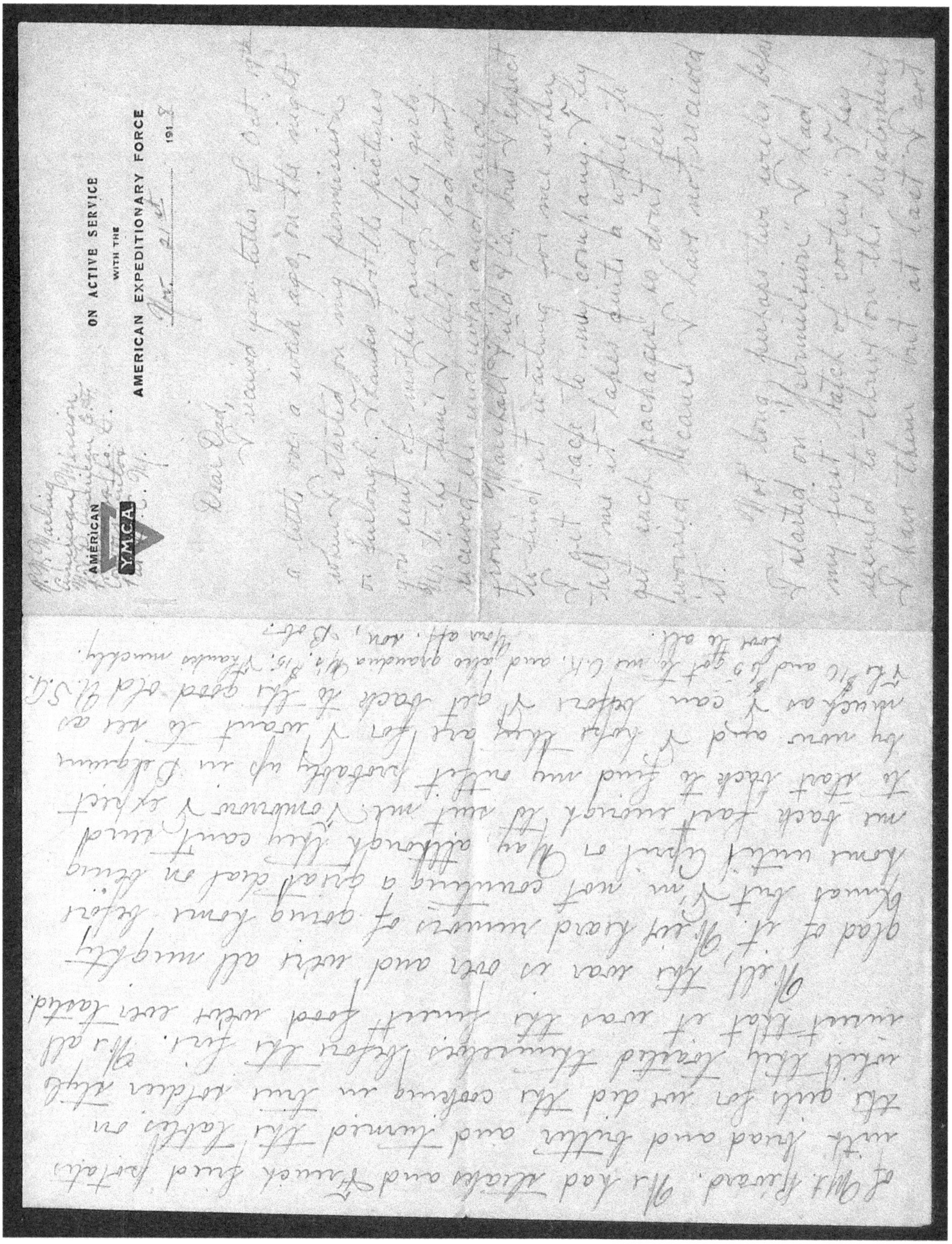
ON ACTIVE SERVICE
WITH THE
AMERICAN EXPEDITIONARY FORCE

AMERICAN Y.M.C.A.

R. W. Marling
American Mission

Nov. 21st 1918

Dear Dad,

I received your letter of Oct. 19th a little over a week ago, on the night when I started on my permission or furlough. Thanks for the pictures you sent of mother and the girls. Up to the time I left I had not received the underwear and candy from Marshall Field & Co. but I expect to find it waiting for me when I get back to my company. They tell me it takes quite a while to get such packages so don't feel worried because I have not received it.

Not long, perhaps two weeks before I started on "permission" I had my first batch of "cooties". They seemed to thrive on the treatment I gave them but at last I got

of Mt. Revard. We had steaks and French fried potatoes with bread and butter and turned the tables on the girls for we did the cooking in true soldier style while they toasted themselves before the fire. We all insist that it was the finest food we've ever tasted.

Well, the war is over and we're all mighty glad of it. We've heard rumors of going home before Xmas but I'm not counting a great deal on being home until April or May although they can't send me back fast enough to suit me. Tomorrow I expect to start back to find my outfit probably up in Belgium by now and I hope they are for I want to see as much as I can before I get back to the good old U.S.A. The $10 and $5 got to me O.K. and also grandma W's $15. Thanks muchly.

Love to all.

Your aff. son,
Bob.

rid of them about two days before starting for Aix les Bains. One thing that I will never forget is Paris the day after the Armistice was signed. I never expect to see another such another happy city in my life. Parades kept forming every minute in every street it seemed, and each grew to enormous proportions before it had gone a block. Captured Hun guns were taken from the Place de la Concorde and wheeled through the streets by Frenchmen, Poilus and Yanks, with French girls perched on the barrels and all over the gun carriage. There was so much excitement that I just had to follow the crowd and consequently did not see a great deal of the city but I will take in all I can on the way back.

Since I have been at Aix I have been having a fine time, sleeping as long as I please, eating as much as I wish, and going and coming when and where I please. And then I have been fortunate in making friends with some of the "Y" girls and they have certainly treated me like a prince. Sergt Mike Driskell of our old ambulance company, Sergt. "Whit" Wright of my present company, three "Y" girls and I have had several wonderful parties together. One afternoon we went up Mt. Revard planning to have a good look at Mt. Blanc but we found ourselves up in the clouds and couldn't see a thing, so we just played around up there in the snow until time to catch the train down the mountain. Another time we had a little "tea party" and violin concert at the girls' hotel and today a picnic on the slopes

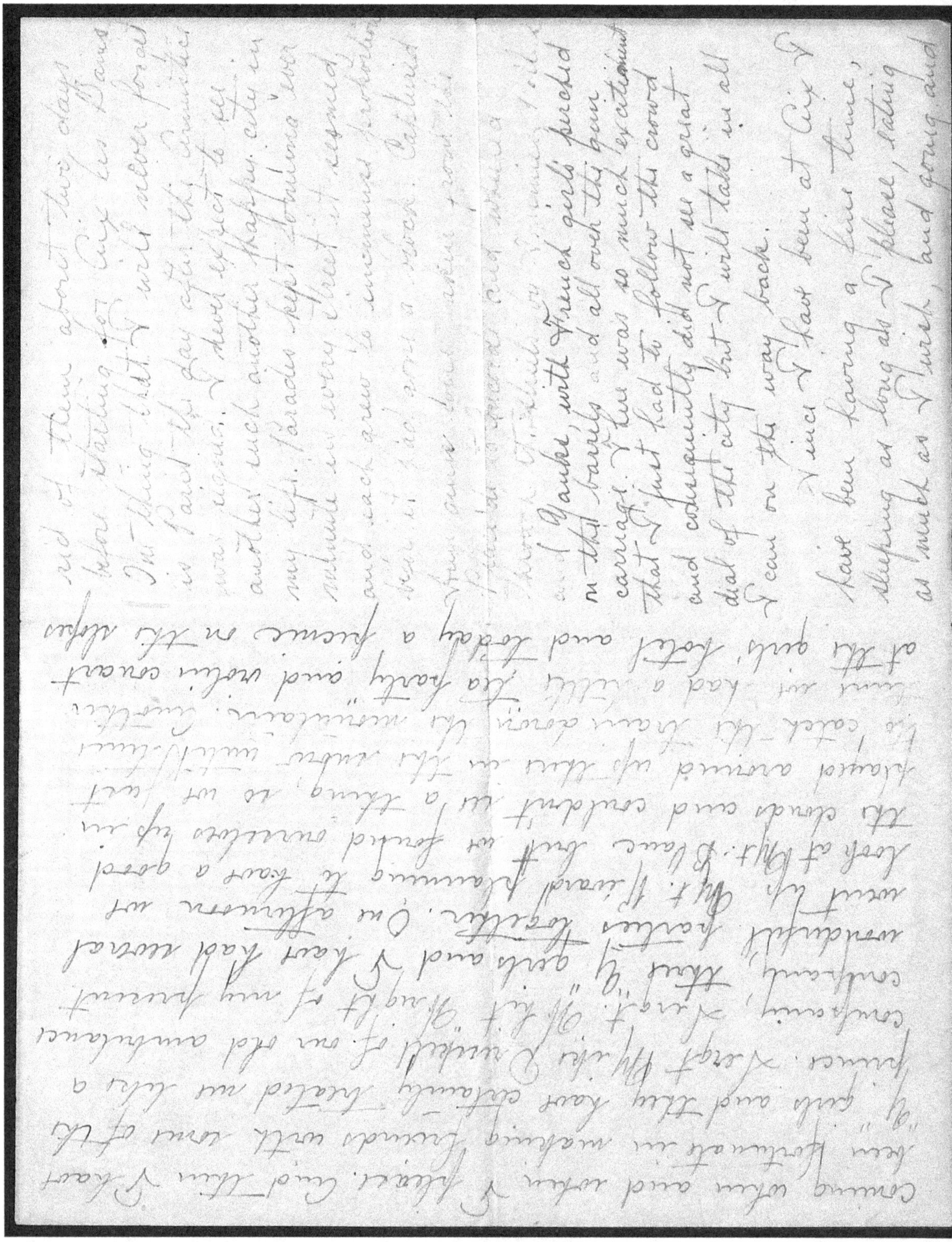
rid of them about two days
before starting for Aix les Bains.
One thing that I will never forget
is Paris the day after the Armistice
was signed. I never expect to see
another such another happy city in
my life. Parades kept forming every
minute in every street it seemed,
and each grew to enormous proportions
before it had gone a block. Captured
Hun guns were taken from the
Place de la Concorde and were drawn
through the streets by Frenchmen, poilus
and Yanks, with French girls perched
on the barrels and all over the gun
carriage. There was so much excitement
that I just had to follow the crowd
and consequently did not see a great
deal of the city but I will take in all
I can on the way back.
Since I have been at Aix I
have been having a fine time,
sleeping as long as I please, eating
as much as I wish, and going and
coming when and when I please. And then I have
been fortunate in making friends with some of the
"Y" girls and they have certainly treated me like a
prince. Sergt Mike Druskell of our old ambulance
company, Sergt. "Whit" Wright of my present
company, three "Y" girls and I have had several
wonderful parties together. One afternoon we
went up Mt. Revard planning to have a good
look at Mt. Blanc but we found ourselves up in
the clouds and couldn't see a thing, so we just
played around up there in the snow until time
to catch the train down the mountain. Another
time we had a little "tea party" and violin concert
at the girls' hotel and today a picnic on the slopes

AMERICAN
Y.M.C.A.
SOLDIER'S
MAIL
Soldier's Mail
U.S. ARMY M.P.E.S. 702
DEC 17 2 PM 1918
Mrs. W. C. Marling
21 Prospect Avenue
Madison
Wisconsin
U.S.A.

Pvt. R. N. Marling
American Mission
M.T.D. American E.F.
Provisional Co. D.
Camion Autos
Par B.C.M.

AMERICAN Y.M.C.A.

ON ACTIVE SERVICE
WITH THE
AMERICAN EXPEDITIONARY FORCE

Dec. 4th, 1918

Dearest Mother,

Time hangs pretty heavily these days when everyone is wondering when his turn will come to go home. We try and try to figure on the day of our probable departure, and just when we think we have it some new rumor comes along and sends our calculations endwise. Some say we will be on the way home by Christmas, others by the last of January etc. but I'll count myself pretty lucky if I am home before the last of April. We still have quite a bit of rolling to do but it is nothing to what it has been up to the time of the Armistice.

just opposite Chattilon sur Marne and the trip I spoke of was one to Rheims, or Reims, as it is spelled over here. That first day I got quite a number of pieces of glass from the windows but could find none from the famous "Rose Window." Later we moved to Reims, but only for a few hours. Then we were moved to Jonchery sur Vesle where we camped for some time. We had a tank convoy that lasted four or five days, one trip a day from Reims to the front. I made the trip the first three days but the fourth I stayed in Reims while some one else took my camion. Old camion #10 hauled her tank up in fine shape but on the way back she caught fire which ended just opposite Chattilon sur Marne and the trip I spoke of was one to Rheims, or Reims, as it is spelled over here. That first day I got quite a number of pieces of glass from the windows but could find none from the famous "Rose Window." Later we moved to Reims, but only for a few hours. Then we were moved to Jonchery sur Vesle where we camped for some time. We had a tank convoy that lasted four or five days, one trip a day from Reims to the front. I made the trip the first three days but the fourth I stayed in Reims while some one else took my camion. Old camion #10 hauled her tank up in fine shape but on the way back she caught fire which ended

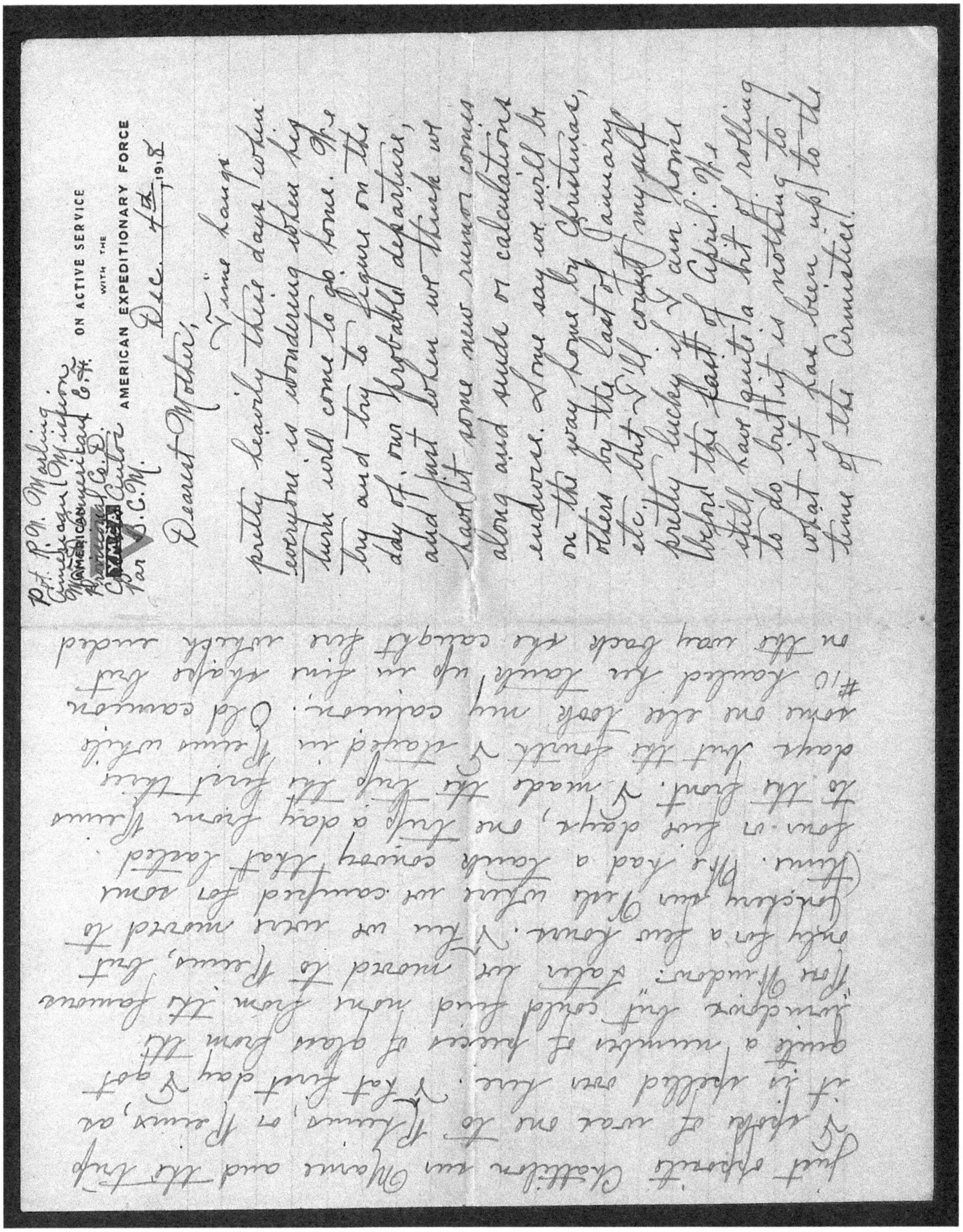
Pvt. R.N. Marling
American Mission
M.T.D. American E.F.
Provisional Co. D.
Convoi Autos
Par B.C.M.

AMERICAN Y.M.C.A.
ON ACTIVE SERVICE
WITH THE
AMERICAN EXPEDITIONARY FORCE

Dec. 4th, 1918

Dearest Mother,

Time hangs pretty heavily these days when everyone is wondering when his turn will come to go home. We try and try to figure on the day of our probable departure, and just when we think we have it some new rumor comes along and sends our calculations endwise. Some say we will be on the way home by Christmas, others by the last of January etc. but I'll count myself pretty lucky if I am home before the last of April. We still have quite a bit of rolling to do but it is nothing to what it has been up to the time of the Armistice.

just opposite Chattilon sur Marne and the trip I spoke of was one to Rheims or Reims, as it is spelled over here. That first day I got quite a number of pieces of glass from the windows but could find none from the famous "Rose Window." Later we moved to Reims, but only for a few hours. Then we were moved to Jonchery sur Vesle where we camped for some time. We had a truck convoy that lasted four or five days, one trip a day from Reims to the front. I made the trip the first three days but the fourth I stayed in Reims while some one else took my column. Old cannon #10 hauled five trucks up in fine shape but on the way back she caught fire which ended

Ever since I came back from Aix I have been trying to shake a nasty cold, but it stubbornly hangs on. Until today I have been keeping myself cooped up and fed up on pills but I think I'll try a change tomorrow and go out on convoy to get some fresh air and a little exercise. If I go, it will be my first time out since November 8th, before going to Aix.

Since I've been back with the outfit we have been stationed near my friends of the old 408th and old ambulance company who are in Groupe Vincent. I've spent several evenings with them and never had a better time. They are a bunch that hang together through everything and can always find the time to get together for a good time. I certainly have missed them, but never have realized how much until just lately. So I have put in an application for a transfer to Co. 367. Kenny Campbell now top sergeant in that company says he has a good job for me.

Your letters have been coming in pretty regularly lately and with others coming in also I am now averaging about one letter a day – more than I can answer I'm afraid. In your letter of Nov. 6th you were wondering where I was. At that time I was at Port a Binson

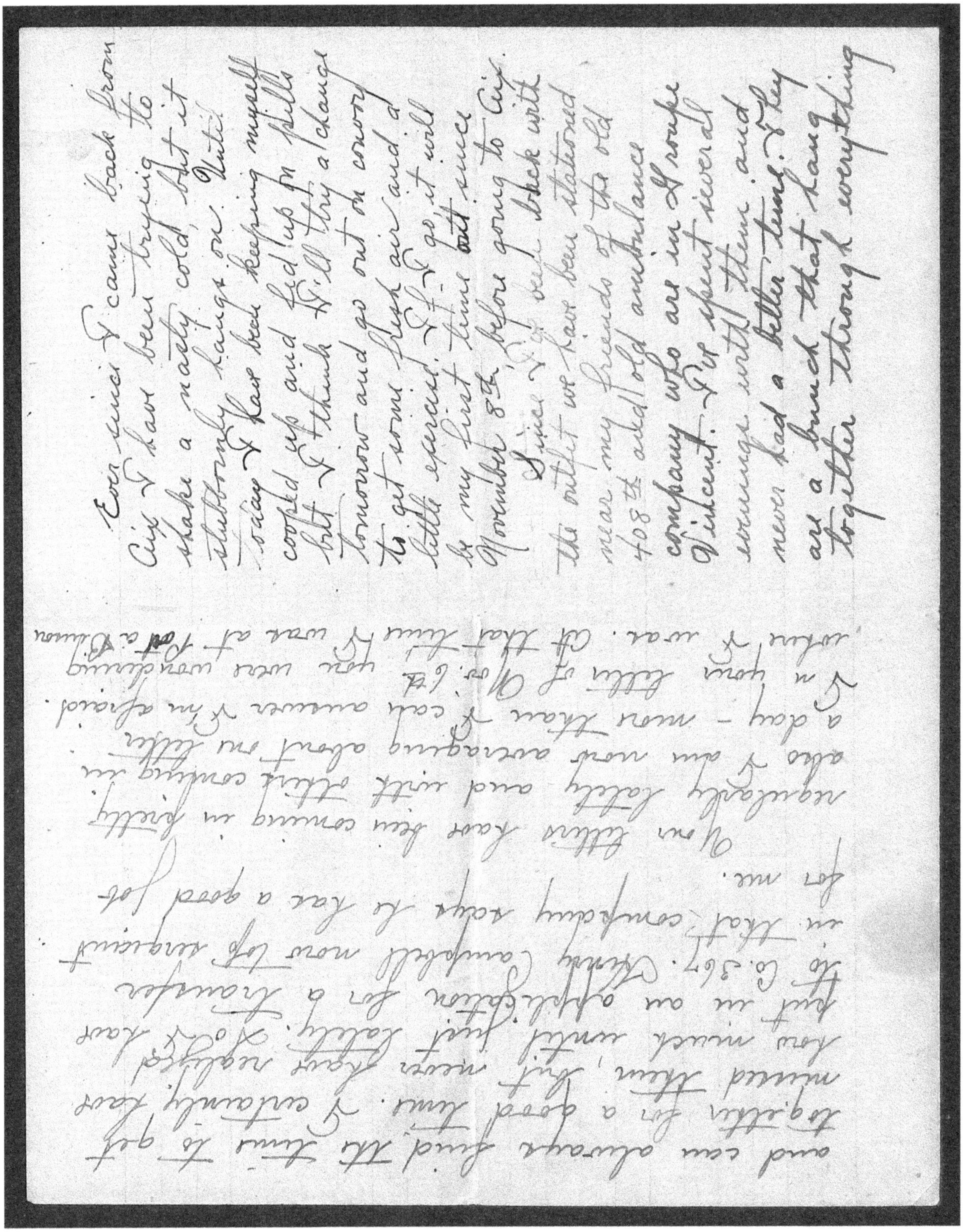

Ever since I came back from
Aix I have been trying to
shake a nasty cold, but it
stubbornly hangs on. Until
today I have been keeping myself
cooped up and fed up on pills
but I think I'll try a change
tomorrow and go out on convoy
to get some fresh air and a
little exercise. If I go, it will
be my first time out since
November 8th, before going to Aix.
Since I've been back with
the outfit we have been stationed
near my friends of the old
408th and old ambulance
company who are in Groupe
Vincent. I've spent several
evenings with them and
never had a better time. They
are a bunch that hang
together through everything
and can always find the time to get
together for a good time. I certainly have
missed them, but never have realized
how much until just lately. So I have
put in an application for a transfer
to Co. 367. Kirby Campbell now top sergeant
in that company says he has a good job
for me.
Your letters have been coming in pretty
regularly lately and with others coming in
also I am now averaging about one letter
a day - more than I can answer I'm afraid.
In your letter of Nov. 6th you were wondering
where I was. At that time I was at Port a Binson

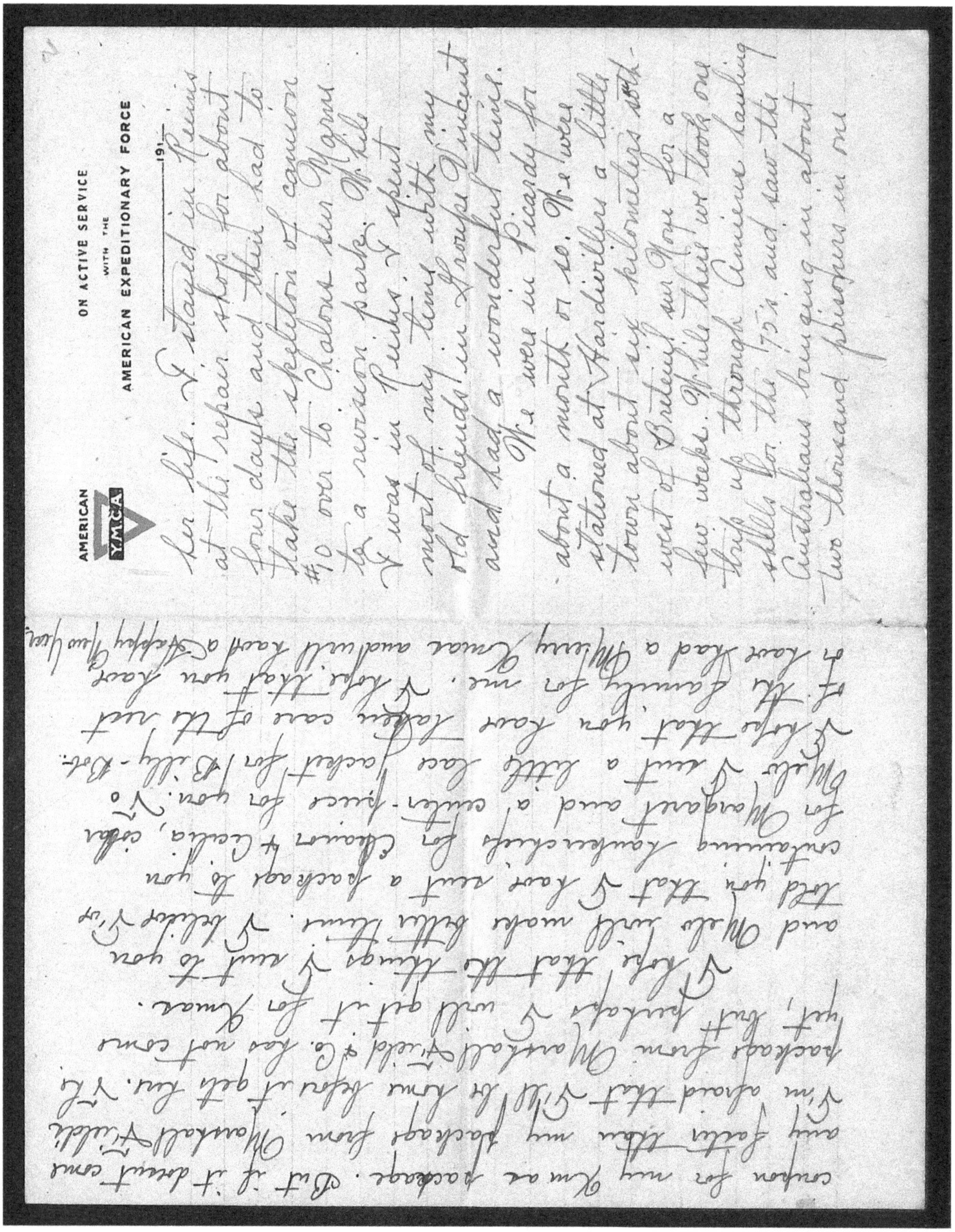
AMERICAN Y.M.C.A.

ON ACTIVE SERVICE WITH THE AMERICAN EXPEDITIONARY FORCE

_______191_

her life. I stayed in Reims at the repair shop for about four days and then had to take the skeleton of camion #10 over to Chalons sur Marne to a revision park. While I was in Reims I spent most of my time with my old friends in Groupe Vincent and had a wonderful time.

We were in Picardy for about a month or so. We were stationed at Hardivillers a little town about six kilometers sothwest of Breteuil sur Noye for a few weeks. While there we took one trip up through Amiens hauling shells for the 75's and saw the Australians bringing in about two thousand prisoners in one

coupon for my Xmas package. But if it doesnt come any faster than my package from Marshall Field's I'm afraid that I'll be home before it gets here. The package from Marshall Field & Co. has not come yet, but perhaps I will get it for Xmas.

I hope that the things I sent to you and Melo will make better time. I believe I've told you that I have sent a package to you containing hankerchiefs for Eleanor & Cecilia, collar for Margaret and a center-piece for you. To Melo I sent a little lace jacket for Billy-Bob. I hope that you have taken care of the rest of the family for me. I hope that you have or have had a Merry Xmas and will have a Happy New Year.

AMERICAN Y.M.C.A.

ON ACTIVE SERVICE
WITH THE
AMERICAN EXPEDITIONARY FORCE

191

her life. I stayed in Reims at the repair shop for about four days and then had to take the skeleton of camion #10 over to Chalons sur Marne to a revision park. While I was in Reims I spent most of my time with my old friends in Groupe Vincent and had a wonderful time.

We were in Picardy for about a month or so. We were stationed at Hardivillers a little town about six kilometers south-west of Breteuil sur Noye for a few weeks. While there we took one trip up through Amiens hauling shells for the 75's and saw the Australians bringing in about two thousand prisoners in one

coupon for my Xmas package. But if it doesnt come any faster than my package from Marshall Field's I'm afraid that I'll be home before it gets here. The package from Marshall Field & Co. has not come yet, but perhaps I will get it for Xmas.

I hope that the things I sent to you and Melo will make better time. I believe I've told you that I have sent a package to you containing hankerchiefs for Eleanor & Cecilia, collar for Margaret and a center-piece for you. To Melo I sent a little lace jacket for Billy-Bob. I hope that you have taken care of the rest of the family for me. I hope that you have or have had a Merry Xmas and will have a Happy New Year.

lunch. Mighty interesting to see. We moved from Hardivillers to Bus, a little town about half way between Montdidier and Roye and a little south of the main highway. Look for it on your map. When that drive was about over we moved back to Esquennoy, a town about three or four kilometers north-west of Breteuil. There we had plenty of work to do cleaning up munition dumps for about a week.

From there we took a long jump to Port à Binson just across the Marne from Chattillon. On the way we went through Estrées St. Denis, Pont Ste. Maxence, Senlis, Meaux, La Ferte-Sa Jouarre, Chateau Thierry, Dormans, all towns we had been through before and a very interesting and beautiful trip. I have told you where we went from Port à Binson in following the Champagne drive. About the time of the Armistice we moved to Roberchamp Farm where we stayed for a few hours until they found a place for us at La Malmaison. On my second day there I left for Aix on the night of the tenth of November, rather the eleventh and got to Paris on the twelfth. When I got back to the company it was located at Saulces-Monclin, about twelve kilometers north-east of Rethel, and we are still here. The boys have been going up to Sedan about every day hauling food supplies or "ravitaillement", and I hope to go up there soon.

I am mighty glad that you received my

bunch. Mighty interesting to see. We moved from Hardivillers to Bus, a little town about half way between Montdidier and Roye and a little south of the main highway. Look for it on your map. When that drive was about over we moved back to Esquennoy, a town about three or four kilometers north-west of Breteuil. There we had plenty of work to do cleaning up munition dumps for about a week.

From there we took a long jump to Port a Binson just across the Marne from Chattillon. On the way we went through Estrées St. Denis, Pont Ste. Maxence, Senlis, Meaux, La Ferte-sa Jouarre, Chateau Thierry, Dormans, all towns we had been through before and

a very interesting and beautiful trip. I have told you where we went from Port a Binson in following the Champagne drive. About the time of the armistice we moved to Pokechamp Farm where we stayed for a few hours until they found a place for us at La Malmaison. On my second day there I left for Aix on the night of the tenth of November, rather the eleventh and got to Paris on the twelfth. When I got back to the company it was located at Saulces-Monclin, about twelve kilometers north east of Rethel, and we are still here. The boys have been going up to Sedan about every day hauling food supplies or "ravitaillement", and I hope to go up there soon.

I am mighty glad that you received my

3

AMERICAN Y.M.C.A.

ON ACTIVE SERVICE
WITH THE
AMERICAN EXPEDITIONARY FORCE

191__

You want to know if I can speak French. Well, I can usually ask for what I want and can carry on a limited conversation, but I certainly can not speak the language. However, I can understand pretty well if the words are spoken slowly. I have quite a bit of fun listening to conversations to see how much I can grasp. Some people speak so distinctly and slowly that I can catch nearly everything they say but others are very difficult to understand for they speak in a "patois" that I have never heard before or else the speak too rapidly.

3

AMERICAN Y.M.C.A.

ON ACTIVE SERVICE
WITH THE
AMERICAN EXPEDITIONARY FORCE

_______________ 191__

You want to know if I can speak French. Well, I can usually ask for what I want and can carry on a limited conversation, but I certainly can not speak the language. However, I can understand pretty well if the words are spoken slowly. I have quite a bit of fun listening to conversations to see how much I can grasp. Some people speak so distinctly and slowly that I can catch nearly everything they say but others are very difficult to understand for they speak in a "patois" that I have never heard before or else they speak too rapidly.

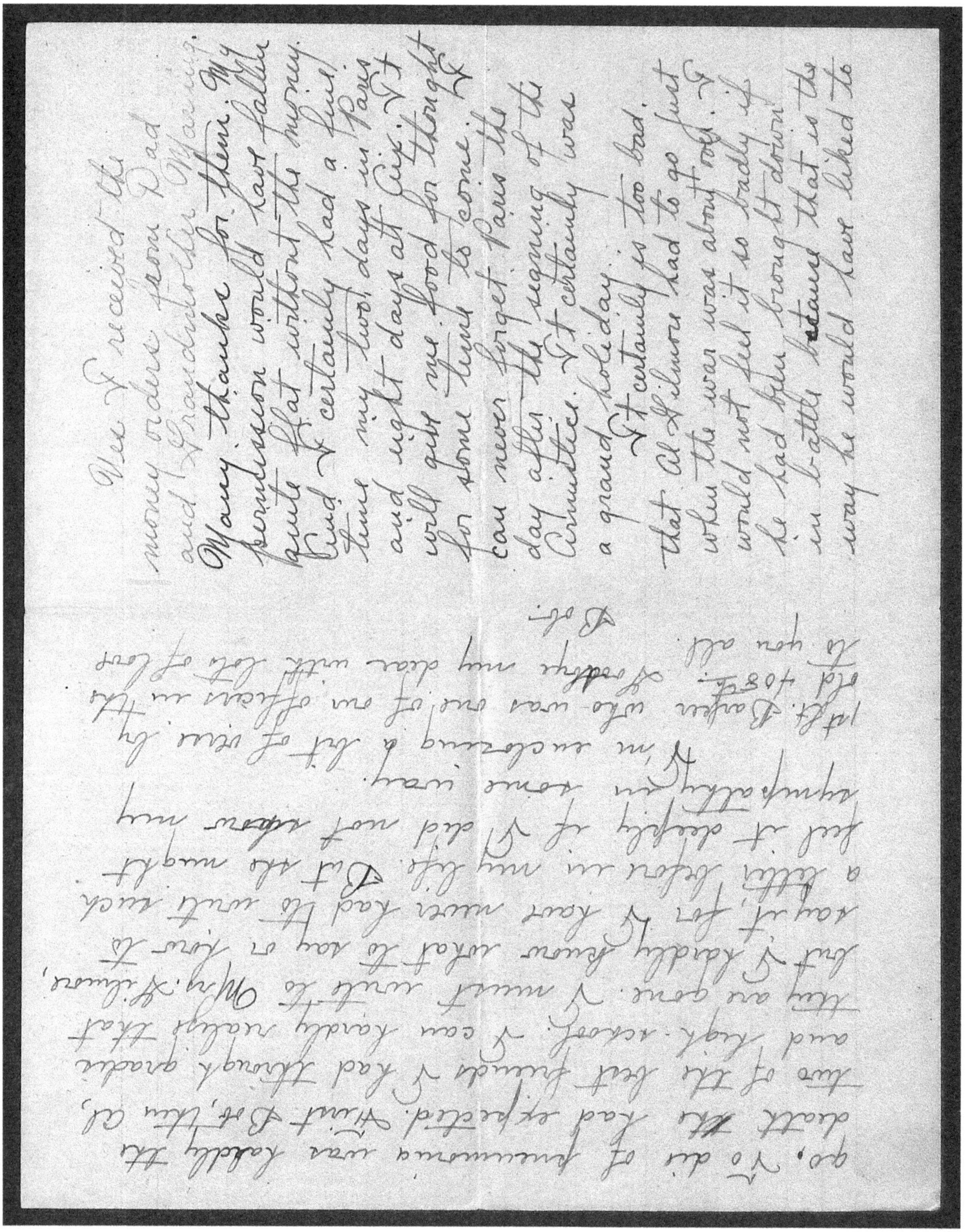

Yes I received the money orders from Dad and Grandmother Waring. Many thanks for them. My permission would have fallen quite flat without the money. And I certainly had a fine time my two days in Paris and eight days at Aix. It will give me food for thought for some time to come. I can never forget Paris the day after the signing of the Armistice. It certainly was a grand holiday.

It certainly is too bad that Al Gilmore had to go just when the war was about over. I would not feel it so badly if he had been brought down in battle because that is the way he would have liked to go. To die of pneumonia was hardly the death he had expected. First Bob, then Al, two of the best friends I had through grades and high-school. I can hardly realize that they are gone. I must write to Mrs. Gilmore, but I hardly know what to say or how to say it, for I have never had to write such a letter before in my life. But she might feel it deeply if I did not show my sympathy in some way.

I'm enclosing a bit of verse by 1st Lt. Barker who was one of our officers in the old 408th. Goodbye my dear with lots of love to you all.

Bob.

Yes I received the money orders from Dad and Grandmother Maring. Many thanks for them. My permission would have fallen quite flat without the money. And I certainly had a fine time my two days in Paris and eight days at Aix. It will give me food for thought for some time to come. I can never forget Paris the day after the signing of the Armistice. It certainly was a grand holiday.

It certainly is too bad that Al Gilmore had to go just when the war was about over. I would not feel it so badly if he had been brought down in battle because that is the way he would have liked to go. To die of pneumonia was hardly the death he had expected. First Bob, then Al, two of the best friends I had through grades and high school. I can hardly realize that they are gone. I must write to Mrs. Gilmore, but I hardly know what to say or how to say it, for I have never had to write such a letter before in my life. But she might feel it deeply if I did not show my sympathy in some way.

I'm enclosing a bit of verse by 1st Lt. Barker who was one of our officers in the old 408th. Goodbye my dear with lots of love to you all.

Bob.

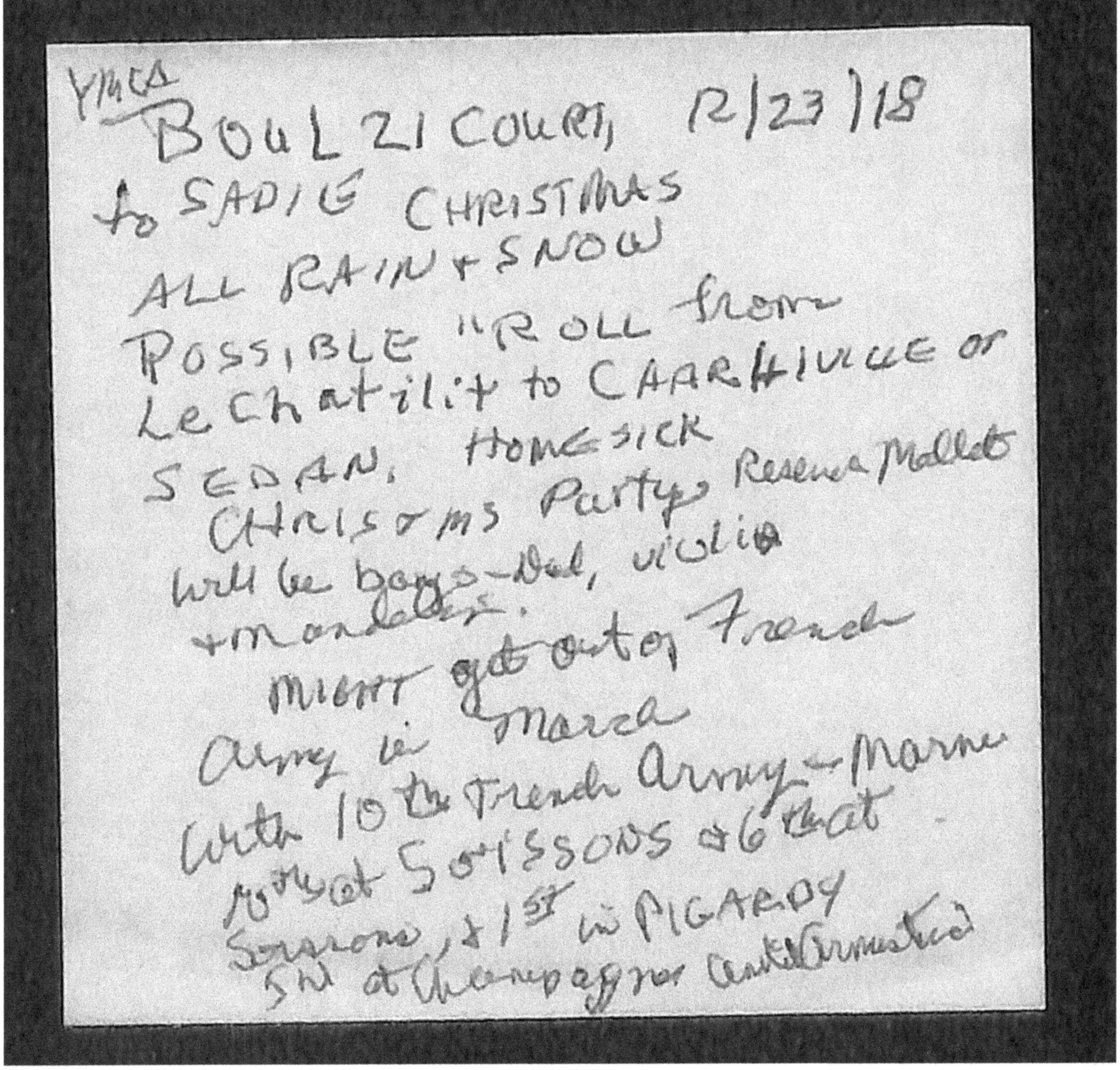
YMCA
BOULZICOURT, 12/23/18
to SADIE CHRISTMAS
ALL RAIN + SNOW
POSSIBLE "ROLL from
Le Chatilit to CAARHIVILLE or
SEDAN, HOMESICK
CHRISTMS Party, Reserve Mallet
will be boys – Dal, violin
+ mandolin.
MIGHT get out of French
Army in March
with 10th French Army – Marne
4th at SOISSONS & 6th at
Soissons, & 1st in PICARDY
5th at Champagne until Armistice

Soldier's Mail
Madison
Wisconsin
U.S.A.

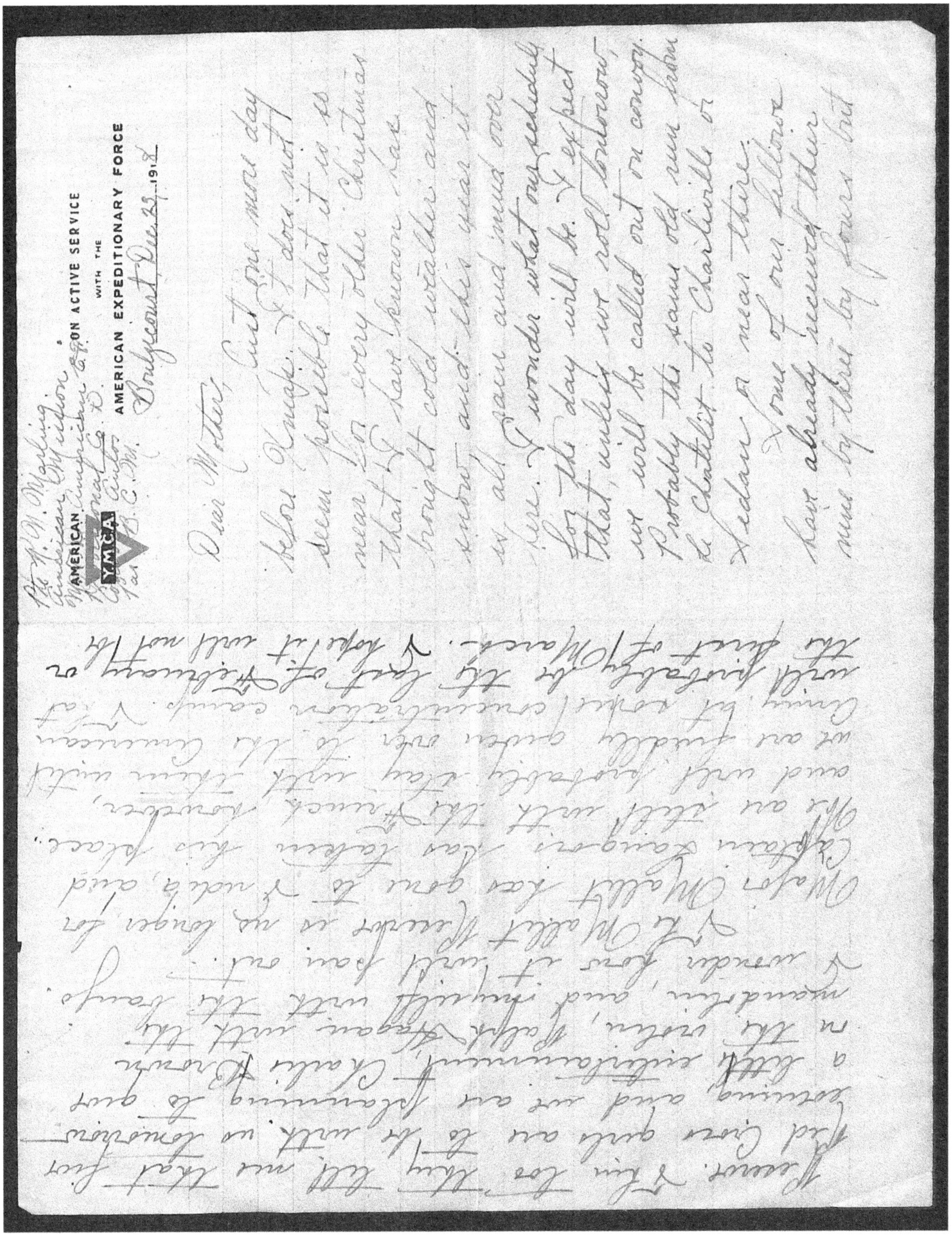

Pte R. W. Marling
American Mission
[illegible] American E.C.
[illegible] Co. D.
[illegible] Autos
1er B.C.M.

AMERICAN Y.M.C.A. ON ACTIVE SERVICE WITH THE AMERICAN EXPEDITIONARY FORCE

Boulzicourt, Dec. 23, 1918

Dear Mother,

Just one more day before Xmas. It does not seem possible that it is so near for every other Christmas that I have known has brought cold weather and snow, and this year it is all rain and mud over here. I wonder what our schedule for the day will be. I expect that, unless we roll tomorrow, we will be called out on convoy. Probably the same old run from Le Chatelet to Charleville or Sedan or near there.

Some of our fellows have already received their nine by three by fours but

Reserve. I hear too they tell me that five Red Cross girls are to be with us tomorrow evening and we are planning to give a little entertainment. Charlie Brown on the violin, Ralph Hagan with the mandolin, and myself with the banjo. I wonder how it will pan out.

Lt. Mallet Reserve is no longer for Major Mallet has gone to Toul, and Captain Langer has taken his place. We are still with the French however, and will probably stay with them until we are finally given over to the American Army by some concentration camp. That will probably be the last of February or the first of March. I hope it will not be

they are here. By the way,
I hear that it is now
possible to send packages
even up to eleven pounds
but don't know how true it
is. I hope that if the
order has gone through and
that you have seen it and
taken advantage of it to
send me some of that
candy you were speaking of
and beaucoup cigarettes.
Cigarettes have been mighty
scarce over here. I haven't
had enough to satisfy me
for about two months and
practically none at all for
the past two weeks.

The latest dope on
going home is that we will
start in six or eight weeks -
possibly less. I hope it is true,

for I surely have a bellyful of France. Tho'
it is a charming country with charming
people, it certainly cannot touch the old
U.S. especially that part of it called
Wisconsin. Funny how a fellow begins
to be lonesome for the old places when
holiday times come around. They are
about the only times that I get really
home-sick. When a fellow gets to thinking
about the good times he has had and
those he is now missing he can't
help but feel a little low.

But they tell me that we are
to have quite a good time here or in
Sedan where the Y.M.C.A is to give
a kind of Christmas Party for the Mallet

AMERICAN
Y.M.C.A.

ON ACTIVE SERVICE
WITH THE
AMERICAN EXPEDITIONARY FORCE

_______________191__

until the latter date for I
go on my second permission
with Whit Wright on the
tenth of February. That will
help to pass the remainder of
my time over here in France.
You ask what division
or regiment I have served with
during the war. I really
cannot tell you for I do not
know, but if it will help you
any I will tell you that
I was with the 10th French
Army while at Soissons,
the 6th French Army at the
Marne (I believe), the 1st Army,
French, in Picardy, and the
5th French Army at the 2nd
Battle of Champagne and
until the armistice was

signed. The engagements that I have been in are as follows
March.- Second Battle of the Somme.
May. - Third Battle of the Aisne.
June.- Defense of Compiegne.
July.- Second Battle of the Marne
Aug.- Third Battle of the Somme
Sept.- Advance North of Compiegne
Oct. Second Battle of Champagne and advance north until signing of the Armistice Nov. 11th 1918.

And would it give you any pleasure to know that Groupement No. 9 (the one your son belongs to) of the Reserve Mallet, is considered the best of any in the entire French Automobile Service? They tell us it is a fact. My date of enlistment was June 9th 1917. Assigned to active duty at Ft. Sheridan on July 13th 1917. The army gives me credit for being a year older than I actually am. I do not know how that happened unless some clerk took it for granted that, because I was with a drafted Bunch, I must be of draft age. They certainly had my correct age when I entered the ambulance company, because while in that organization I saw my service record several times. I believe the mistake must have been made when I entered the 408th or since that time.

Well mother dear I guess I have about run out of things to say so I had better bid you goodnight. I am well and quite contented so do not worry. Love to all and best wishes for luck and happiness in the New Year.

Your affectionate son,
Bob.

www.ingramcontent.com/pod-product-compliance
Lightning Source LLC
Chambersburg PA
CBHW080515090426
42734CB00015B/3063
* 9 7 8 1 6 3 0 1 0 0 1 2 4 *